# Blue Ribbon
# RECIPES

*The Old Farmer's Almanac*

# Blue Ribbon
# RECIPES

Award-Winning Recipes
From America's Country Fairs

The Old Farmer's Almanac Books
Series Editor: Sarah Elder Hale
Consulting Editor: Susan Peery
Manuscript Author: Polly Bannister
Copyeditor: Barbara Jatkola
Proofreader: Jack Burnett
Art Director: Carol Loria

Cover Illustration and Chapter Title Page Art:
Warren Kimble®

Distributed in the book trade by Houghton Mifflin

*The Old Farmer's Almanac*®, North America's oldest continuously published periodical and the original Farmer's Almanac since 1792, is owned and published by:

Yankee Publishing Inc.
1121 Main Street
Dublin, NH 03444

For additional information about *The Old Farmer's Almanac*, visit us on the Web at: www.almanac.com

Second edition

# Contents

Chicken Parmesan Quiche • Healthy, Hot, and Garlicky Wings • Mahony's
Bruschetta • Buttermilk Biscuit Sausage Pinwheels • Mexican Quiche •
Greek Crab Salad • Spinach "Zinger" Salad • Endive Salad with Cherries,
Roquefort, and Walnuts • Beef Insalada

*Central Maine Egg Festival, Pittsfield, Maine • Iowa State Fair, Des Moines,
Iowa • Spinach Festival, Lenexa, Kansas • National Cherry Festival,
Traverse City, Michigan*

Real Louisiana Gumbo • Creamy Crab Bisque • Hungarian Garden
Vegetable Chicken Soup • White Oyster Chili • Pumpkin Tortilla Soup •
Garlic Mushroom Soup • Tried-and-True Beef Stew

*Gumbo Festival, Bridge City, Louisiana • St. Mary's Oyster Festival,
Leonardtown, Maryland • Pumpkin Festival, Morton, Illinois • Gilroy Garlic
Festival, Gilroy, California*

# Foreword

For the past hundred years or so, recipes have represented a healthy portion of the editorial fare in *The Old Farmer's Almanac*. This was an evolutionary process, however. The Almanac was originally written to provide farmers with astronomical information, weather forecasts, and practical (mostly agricultural) advice. The only food-related features during the 1790s, for instance, were those such as "The Art of Making Cheese" and "To Refine Sugar." The first real recipe didn't appear until the 1800 edition. After describing "how to roast a piece of beef," it provided instructions for making an onion sauce: "Put them into a clean sauce-pan with a good piece of butter, a little salt, and a gill of sweet cream; stir them over the fire."

From then on, recipes and cooking advice became an increasingly large segment of every Almanac. Today, when we feature a recipe contest, we receive hundreds of original recipes from all over the United States and Canada. From these, we not only select the winners, but we also use some of them in our various features on food-related topics. Similarly, the blue-ribbon recipes in this book, created by winning cooks all across the country, are the crème de la crème from county and state fairs and other cook-offs.

We trust our readers for accuracy, originality, and "goodness" of taste and consistency. But we also test each recipe ourselves prior to publication. (This policy began some 30 years ago following our publication of an untested recipe for cream of tartar biscuits, which, we were told, produced something very similar to small cakes of cement.) These days, about once a month, usually on a Monday, the wonderful aromas of Almanac foods permeate our offices in Dublin, New Hampshire, when our recipe testers deliver the dishes they've cooked the previous weekend. It's then the duty of all of us who work for the Almanac to sample each dish and offer an opinion. I don't recall uttering a single negative comment during the several Mondays when the recipes contained in this book were tested.

# What is *The Old Farmer's Almanac?*

First of all, it's the oldest continuously published periodical in North America. It was established in 1792 by Robert B. Thomas, a Massachusetts schoolteacher whose name and likeness still appear on the familiar yellow cover, and it has been a part of the American scene in every year since.

Like any publication legitimately calling itself an almanac, it is also, as such books were known in ancient times, a "calendar of the heavens." In other words, one of its primary duties is to provide on a daily basis the astronomical structure of the coming year—the rise and set times of the Sun, Moon, and planets; conjunctions; eclipses; and so forth.

Perhaps what *The Old Farmer's Almanac* is most of all, however, is a vast compendium of useful and entertaining information. Its major subjects include food, gardening, weather, home remedies, history, and odd facts that you just won't find anywhere else. A feature section covering current consumer tastes and trends—from collectibles to fashions to health news to money-saving ideas to, well, just about everything going on in America—helps ensure that each edition stands as a time capsule of the year. Even though the name is "old," each edition is brand-new.

In recent years, the circulation of *The Old Farmer's Almanac* has skyrocketed to 18 million. (Robert B. printed and sold 3,000 copies of the first edition.) So, in addition to being America's oldest publication, perhaps it has become America's most beloved publication as well.

JUDSON D. HALE SR.
Editor in Chief
*The Old Farmer's Almanac*
(The 12th editor since 1792)

# Introduction

T hroughout the year, across America, fairs, food festivals, cook-offs, bake-offs, national cooking competitions, and brand-name sweepstakes are held. Many of these celebrations, like the Garlic Festival in Gilroy, California, and the Mushroom Festival in Kennett Square, Pennsylvania, honor local harvests. Others, like the Seafood Festival in Charlestown, Rhode Island, pay tribute to a coastal industry. State and county fairs celebrate our agricultural heritage. At festival time, communities gather together to enjoy parades, concerts, beauty pageants, craft shows, cooking contests, and other competitions—from livestock and rodeo to mashed potato wrestling and cherry picking. The highlight of these fairs and festivals is the food—not fried dough and pizza from the midway concessions, but the food entered in cooking competitions.

Cakes, pies, biscuits, jams, pickles, and more, freshly prepared with love and pride, are loaded in cars at dawn by cooks hoping for a blue ribbon. Many of these recipes are original, achieved after hours of experimentation. Others have been passed down through generations or come right off the Certo box, but are nonetheless presented with a flair and care that judges look for. In this cookbook, we have gathered together championship recipes from cooks around the country. These recipes have made the grade in flavor, texture, appearance, and presentation and are fondly remembered long after the last bit is eaten.

With the recipes come the cooks—people who appreciate delicious food, presented well and eaten in good company. They share more than their recipes; they share their stories. Becky Quinn of Springfield, Missouri, learned to can at her grandmother's side in the warm kitchen of the farm her family homesteaded. Every summer for nearly 40 years, Becky has put up Grandmother Lida Quinn's Pickled Beets. Morris Shanstrom of Pueblo, Colorado, loved cooking from the first bread he saw baked by the cook his family took in during the Depression. He and his wife made cooking a family activity and with their two children have given cooking demonstrations for 4-H groups and local TV shows. In 1996, they traveled to New York City to share prizewinning recipes with America's great chefs at the annual tribute to James Beard to benefit Citymeals-on-Wheels. Larry Mitchell of Caldwell, Idaho, was cooking supper for his children when he discovered he was out of tortillas; he substituted baked potatoes, and the potato fajita was born.

Here prizewinning cooks tell us the little things that make a difference, such as fresh herbs or a perfectly ripe tomato, and they enjoy the challenge of getting it right. Reverend Monsignor J. Anthony Luminais from the Gumbo Festival in Bridge City, Louisiana, shares his mother's recipe and tells us that the secret is in the gumbo "filé"—powdered sassafras leaves. Members of his Catholic Youth Organization harvest the leaves, dry them, and then pulverize them with rolling pins. Mary Ann Brahler from the Flemington Agricultural Fair in New Jersey makes Violet Infusion Jelly with pesticide-free violets. On golden summer days, Mary Ann can be found picking violets by the bushel at an abandoned farm near her home. Doris Laska of Winona, Minnesota, has won numerous blue ribbons for her dill pickles made with homegrown midget cucumbers. Each morning in the weeks before the Minnesota State Fair, Doris heads out to her garden and carefully selects small, uniform cucumbers, always leaving a bit of the stem on for the perfect look.

This cookbook is a tribute to the hard work of these cooks and others across the country. It is a celebration of America's bounty and the many hands that bring it to our tables. Our hearty thanks to agricultural and home arts superintendents, festival chairpersons, volunteers, chambers of commerce, our recipe testers, and great cooks and good eaters the country over.

# Preface

## How to Win a Blue Ribbon

Have you ever thought about entering one of your creations in a cooking contest? Maybe you have, only to find out that, as in any competition, it takes strategy and perseverance to win a blue ribbon.

After talking to hundreds of winning cooks, we have determined that there are ways to improve your chances of getting that blue ribbon. These cooks all have one important quality: determination. That means having the discipline (and time) to make a hundred cookies to get six that look just right or to bake a dozen pies to get one with a picture-perfect crust. We talked to several winners who make sure they have enough preparation time by scheduling a vacation during the competition.

Most of the winners we know enter lots of recipes in many different categories and change their recipes according to the judges' comments. The following year, they enter the modified recipes as well as a few new ones in different categories. Winning cooks spend hours experimenting and refining techniques. Tammy Reiss of Moore, Oklahoma, says that her apple jelly (see page 141) wins because "it is crystal clear," and to ensure this she strains the fruit through three or four layers of cheesecloth. Also, she religiously skims off the foam, despite the fact that many apple jelly recipes call for adding butter to avoid this step. She told us that the one time she added butter, her jelly was cloudy and did not win a blue ribbon, so the next year she returned to skimming.

Winning cooks try to catch the judges' eyes. Their recipes are original, yet they stay within the contest parameters. For example, if they are making a two-crust pie, they use an unusual fruit, such as pears or persimmons, and they design a part-solid, part-lattice crust. To ensure a good look, entrants often add a garnish, such as fresh berries, at the last minute to prevent "bleeding."

When sending a recipe to a cook-off, winning cooks pay particular attention to how it is written. They use letter-size paper (not an index card unless the contest rules require this) and type or print neatly. They list the ingredients (spelled correctly) in the order they are used, with no abbreviations for measures. If the recipe calls for a can or package, they indicate the size in ounces: 1 can (12 ounces) tomatoes. Entrants also need to be specific about pan size, greased or ungreased, cooking temperature and time, and yield.

A winning recipe at any cook-off combines ordinary, easy-to-find ingredients to create a unique taste. According to officials from more than 100 cooking contests, including the Pillsbury Bake-off and the Idaho Beef Cook-off, judges look for a dish that has an addictive taste and pleasing texture, photographs well, and can be prepared in 30 minutes or less using no more than ten ingredients. Sponsors also want their products presented prominently.

When judges rate a prepared entry, taste is the most important criterion. Forty percent of the score is normally allotted for taste. Not only does a winning entry have to taste good, but its flavor also must have wide appeal. For instance, "spicy" means different things in different regions. A large amount of fiery jalapeños will doom a recipe unless a milder substitute, such as canned chilies, is offered. (Of course, if the contest sponsor makes the spicy ingredient, use it.) In general, judges like to see three or four seasonings added to ten or fewer main ingredients.

At most country fairs, the winner receives a ribbon and not much (if any) prize money. In larger contests sponsored by product manufacturers, cooks can win thousands of dollars, an exotic trip, a designer kitchen, a new appliance, or a lifetime supply of a particular product. Some cooks view entering cook-offs as a career. Others are encouraged to enter a specific contest by family members who love a particular recipe and are sure it is a winner. Whatever the motivation, these hardworking cooks have our admiration for the hours that go into their winning recipes.

# Chapter 1

## Appetizers & Salads

# Central Maine Egg Festival

### Pittsfield, Maine

F or over 30 years, Pittsfield has been celebrating central Maine's brown egg production with the annual Central Maine Egg Festival. Held on the fourth Saturday of July, the festival is a combination of old home week and county fair, regularly attracting about 25,000 people. Activities include an early-bird breakfast (a total of 4,000 eggs are cooked in a 10-foot-diameter frying pan), a mile-long parade, continuous free entertainment on two stages, a scholarship pageant, horseshoe pitching, and fireworks. Egg events include the search for the world's largest chicken egg, with entries coming from as far away as Poland, Korea, and Mexico. Quiche and cheesecake contests are a festival highlight.

# Chicken Parmesan Quiche

*10 appetizer servings*

1 whole boneless, skinless chicken breast, halved
2 tablespoons chicken broth
2 tablespoons burgundy
½ cup chunky spaghetti sauce
Pastry for single-crust 9-inch pie
¾ cup shredded mozzarella cheese, divided
¼ cup plus 2 tablespoons freshly grated Parmesan cheese, divided
4 eggs
1¼ cups light cream
⅛ teaspoon freshly ground black pepper
½ cup Italian-style bread crumbs
¼ teaspoon paprika
2 tablespoons butter

**Cut** the chicken into small pieces and sauté lightly in a skillet with the broth and burgundy. Cook until the meat is done but not browned. Drain the juices from the pan and add the spaghetti sauce. Let cool for about 20 minutes in the refrigerator.

**Preheat** the oven to 400° F. Line a 9-inch pie plate with the pastry. Put the chicken mixture in the crust and cover with ½ cup of the mozzarella and ¼ cup of the Parmesan. In a small bowl, beat the eggs thoroughly. Add the cream and pepper. Pour over the cheese. Bake for about 30 minutes, or until a light golden brown.

**Meanwhile,** in a small bowl, combine the bread crumbs, remaining ¼ cup mozzarella, remaining 2 tablespoons Parmesan, and paprika. Cut in the butter with two knives or use a food processor equipped with a pastry blade. Sprinkle over the cooked quiche and return to the oven for 10 minutes, or until the quiche is set.

Patrice Allen, Pittsfield, Maine
*Quiche Contest, Central Maine Egg Festival,*
*Pittsfield, Maine*

# Healthy, Hot, and Garlicky Wings

*4 to 5 appetizer servings*

2 pounds chicken wings (approximately 15 wings)
3 heads garlic
1 cup plus 1 tablespoon olive oil
10 to 15 drops Tabasco
1 cup freshly grated Parmesan cheese
1 cup Italian-style bread crumbs
1 teaspoon freshly ground black pepper

**Preheat** the oven to 375° F. Disjoint the chicken wings, discarding the tips. Rinse and pat dry with a paper towel.

**Separate** the garlic cloves and peel. Place the garlic, 1 cup of the oil, and Tabasco in a blender or food processor and purée. Pour the purée into a shallow bowl.

**Combine** the Parmesan, bread crumbs, and pepper in a large plastic bag. Dip the wings, one at a time, in the garlic purée, then shake or roll in the bread crumb mixture, coating thoroughly. Coat two shallow nonstick baking pans with the remaining 1 tablespoon oil. Arrange the wings in a single layer in the pans. Avoid having the wings touch each other. Drizzle with the remaining garlic purée and sprinkle with the leftover bread crumb mixture. Bake for 45 to 60 minutes, or until browned, then place under the broiler for a few minutes until crisp.

Winifred Harano, Los Angeles, California
*Gilroy Garlic Festival, Gilroy, California*

# Mahony's Bruschetta

6 servings

1 loaf French or Italian bread without seeds
10 large cloves garlic, peeled
¾ cup olive oil (preferably extra-virgin)
1½ cups whipping cream
½ cup grated good-quality Romano cheese
½ cup freshly grated Parmesan cheese (preferably imported Italian)
3 tablespoons butter
1 tablespoon chopped fresh parsley
Paprika

**Preheat** the oven to 350° F. Cut the bread diagonally into 1-inch slices without cutting through the bottom crust. In a blender or food processor equipped with a steel blade, finely chop the garlic. With the processor running, add the oil to make a thin paste. Slather the garlic paste on the cut surfaces and top and side crusts of the bread. Bake directly on the oven rack (with a pan on the rack below to catch drippings) for 10 to 12 minutes, or until the top is crisp.

**While** the bread is in the oven, heat the cream in a heavy saucepan. Do not boil.

**Stir** in the Romano and Parmesan slowly so that the sauce is absolutely smooth (a wire whisk works well). Stir in the butter and keep the sauce warm until the bread is ready.

**When everyone is seated** at the table, place the bread in a warm, shallow serving dish with sides. Cut through the bottom crust and pour the sauce over the bread. Sprinkle with the parsley and paprika and serve immediately.

Neil Mahony, Ventura, California
*Gilroy Garlic Festival, Gilroy, California*

# Iowa State Fair

## Des Moines, Iowa

The Iowa State Fair is one of the oldest and largest agricultural expositions in the United States. It was the inspiration for Phil Stong's award-winning novel *State Fair* (University of Iowa Press, 1996; originally published 1932), and in recent years it has seen an annual attendance of more than one million visitors. The fair, held for 11 days in mid-August, boasts one of the largest livestock shows in the country. A fair highlight is a life-size dairy cow sculpted out of more than a quarter ton of butter by Norma Duffield Lyon. She fashions it by hand in about 16 hours, working in a refrigerated room. The sculpture is then displayed in a 40° F showcase in the Agriculture Building. "Duffy" gained national fame in 1994 by sculpting a 400-pound likeness of country singer Garth Brooks out of butter.

During the course of the fair, families from across the state vacation at the fair campgrounds, relaxing in the shade of century-old hickory, oak, and walnut trees.

# Buttermilk Biscuit Sausage Pinwheels

*8 servings*

½ cup shortening
2 cups self-rising flour
1 cup buttermilk
1 pound bulk pork sausage

**In a medium bowl,** cut the shortening into the flour with a pastry blender (or use a food processor). Add the buttermilk and mix. On a lightly floured surface, knead the dough for a few seconds, adding additional flour if it is too sticky. Roll out into a 9x12-inch rectangle. Spread the sausage over the dough. Roll up like a jelly roll, starting from the short side of the rectangle. Chill for 30 minutes.

**Preheat** the oven to 425° F. Cut the chilled dough into ½-inch slices. Place, cut side down, on a lightly greased baking sheet. Bake for 25 to 30 minutes, or until lightly browned and the sausage is completely cooked.

Nancy Tuttle, Winterset, Iowa
*Iowa State Fair, Des Moines, Iowa*

# Mexican Quiche

*12 appetizer servings*

Pastry for single-crust 10-inch pie
½ cup shredded Cheddar cheese
1 tablespoon olive oil
1 medium onion, chopped
1 small green bell pepper, chopped
2 cloves garlic, minced
1 small tomato, diced
7 black olives, sliced
5 ounces (½ package) frozen corn
2 teaspoons chili powder
1 teaspoon ground cumin
1 teaspoon dried oregano
Pinch of salt
Pinch of freshly ground black pepper
6 eggs
1 pint whipping cream
Sour cream and picante sauce for garnish

**TIP**

*Blue Ribbon*

★ ★ ★ ★ ★

**S**alt toughens eggs. Add it to egg dishes only after they are cooked. Egg dishes should be cooked at low or moderate heat, or they'll toughen.

**Preheat** the oven to 350° F. Line a 10-inch pie plate with the pastry. Sprinkle the cheese on the crust.

**Heat** the oil in a skillet and sauté the onion, pepper, garlic, tomato, olives, and corn. When soft, add the chili powder, cumin, oregano, salt, and pepper. Spread over the cheese in the pie plate.

**In a medium bowl,** beat the eggs until light and frothy. Add the cream and mix well. Pour over the vegetable mixture. Bake for 1 hour and 10 minutes, or until firm in the center. Garnish with sour cream and picante sauce before serving.

Sherry Morrell, Waterville, Maine
*Quiche Contest, Central Maine Egg Festival,*
*Pittsfield, Maine*

# Greek Crab Salad

*6 servings*

*Salad*

1 to 2 heads romaine lettuce
1 cucumber, sliced
1 small red onion, thinly sliced
2 large ripe tomatoes, cut into wedges
½ green bell pepper, sliced

*Dressing*

½ cup olive oil
¼ cup red wine vinegar
½ teaspoon salt
1 teaspoon minced dried oregano
Freshly ground black pepper, to taste
1 pound lump crabmeat
12 Greek black olives
4 ounces feta cheese, crumbled

**To make the salad,** tear the lettuce into bite-size pieces and place in a large bowl. Add the cucumber, onion, tomatoes, and pepper. Set aside.

**To make the dressing,** in a small bowl, combine the oil, vinegar, salt, oregano, and pepper. Mix well. Pour over the salad and toss. Divide the salad among six salad plates and top each with a portion of crabmeat, olives, and cheese. Serve immediately.

Alma Madanick, Chincoteague, Virginia
*National Hard Crab Derby,*
*Crisfield, Maryland*

# SPINACH FESTIVAL

~

Lenexa, Kansas

Lenexa holds its annual Spinach Festival in early September. Activities include making the largest spinach salad in the world, portions of which are sold to festival-goers; a spinach café, where all sorts of tasty spinach dishes are served; and a craft and antique show where people display and sell their work and collectibles. The Lenexa Historical Society sponsors the event, which pays tribute to a bygone farming era. During the 1920s and 1930s, Belgian truck farmers filled Chicago canneries with spinach grown in Lenexa. It is said that their secret was soil made rich by manure from the Kansas City stockyards.

# Spinach "Zinger" Salad

*6 servings*

According to Joan Walters. "Not only is this a beautifully colored and delicious salad, but any remaining dressing will keep well in the refrigerator and can be reheated as additional salad is prepared."

## Salad

½ pound fresh spinach, washed, stemmed, and cut into horizontal strips
3 medium oranges, peeled, cleaned of all membrane, sectioned,
　　seeded, and cut into pieces (approximately 4 pieces per orange slice)
½ cup dry roasted peanuts

## Dressing

4 eggs (or egg substitute equivalent to 4 eggs)
¼ cup dry mustard
1 scant cup sugar
2 teaspoons salt
2 cups heavy cream, divided
⅔ cup white vinegar

**To make the salad,** in a large bowl, combine the spinach, orange pieces, and peanuts. Cover and refrigerate until thoroughly chilled.

**To make the dressing,** in a medium bowl, beat the eggs well. Add the mustard, sugar, and salt; beat again. Slowly add 1 cup of the cream and vinegar. Pour into a medium saucepan and cook over low heat until thickened. Remove from the heat. Add the remaining 1 cup cream, whisking to combine well. Serve the well-chilled salad with the hot dressing in a small pitcher on the side.

Joan Walters, Lenexa, Kansas
*Spinach Festival, Lenexa, Kansas*

# Endive Salad with Cherries, Roquefort, and Walnuts

*4 to 6 servings*

**1 small head endive, rinsed and drained**
**1 small head butter lettuce, rinsed and drained**
**¾ cup walnut oil**
**3 tablespoons sherry wine vinegar**
**1 tablespoon lemon juice**
**Salt and pepper, to taste**
**½ cup walnuts, toasted**
**½ cup fresh sweet cherries, rinsed and pitted**
**4 ounces Roquefort cheese, crumbled**
**2 tablespoons minced fresh chives**

**Tear** the endive and lettuce into bite-size pieces and place in a salad bowl. In a small bowl, combine the walnut oil, vinegar, and lemon juice. Beat with a wire whisk until well blended. Season with salt and pepper to taste. Drizzle over the greens and mix well. Arrange the greens on individual salad plates and top each serving with a portion of toasted walnuts, cherries, Roquefort cheese, and chives.

Joy Cassens, Traverse City, Michigan
*National Cherry Festival, Traverse City, Michigan*

# NATIONAL CHERRY FESTIVAL

Traverse City, Michigan

Traverse City has been home to the National Cherry Festival for more than 75 years. Michigan produces 70 percent of the world's cherries. For a week in early July, you can find just-picked sweet cherries everywhere in the Grand Traverse Bay area. Pie-eating contests for children and adults are held every day. You also can attend the Taste of Cherries Food Fair or the Grand Cherry Buffet Luncheon. Or you may opt for an orchard tour, where you can eat all the cherries you pick!

# Beef Insalada

*4 servings*

1 pound rare roast beef (deli-style works well), thinly sliced
    and cut into strips
½ cup Caesar salad dressing
1 can (15 ounces) chickpeas, drained
1 can (15 ounces) red beans, rinsed and drained
1 small red onion, thinly sliced into rings
1 jar (6½ ounces) marinated artichoke hearts with marinade
8 soft bread sticks
1 bag (12 ounces) chopped romaine lettuce
    (or 1 head, chopped)

**In a large bowl,** combine the roast beef, salad dressing, chickpeas, red beans, onion, and artichoke hearts. Toss gently, cover, and refrigerate for 30 minutes.

**Before serving,** lightly toast the bread sticks according to the package directions. Place the lettuce on a serving platter and spoon the beef mixture on top. Serve with the toasted bread sticks.

Maya Kline, Boise, Idaho
*Idaho Beef Cook-off, Boise, Idaho*

　For kitchen tips and more recipes, go to www.almanac.com/food.

# Chapter 2

## Soups & Stews

# Gumbo Festival

## Bridge City, Louisiana

Monsignor Luminais tells us that this recipe comes from his mother, who served gumbo and potato salad every Sunday for dinner throughout his childhood. He attributes the success of the recipe to the oyster water. In 1973, when his Holy Guardian Angels Church needed to raise funds for a new building, the parish started the Gumbo Festival. Every year since then, Bridge City, now known as the "Gumbo Capital of the World," hosts the festival in October. Activities include a 5k run over the Huey P. Long Bridge, continuous live entertainment, and a gumbo-cooking contest. More than 2,000 gallons of seafood and chicken/sausage gumbo are served during the three-day festival. The Catholic Youth Organization raises money by selling hundreds of jars of gumbo filé. They make the filé by picking sassafras leaves from local trees, drying the leaves in the sun, and then placing the dried leaves in pillowcases and pulverizing them with rolling pins.

# Real Louisiana Gumbo

*8 main-course servings*

This gumbo freezes well. If you are planning to freeze it, do so before adding the oysters. When you're ready to serve the gumbo, defrost it and continue on with the recipe. (Note: Oyster water is the liquid left from shucking oysters and can usually be purchased at a fish market. If you cannot obtain fresh oyster water, use 1 gallon chicken stock or water.)

1 gallon oyster water
1 cup roux (equal parts flour and oil)
1 cup chopped onion
1 cup chopped celery
1 cup chopped green bell pepper
1 cup chopped fresh parsley
5 pounds hen, cut into large pieces
2 pounds andouille (smoked sausage made
    with pork and garlic), cut into
    bite-size pieces
1 gallon oysters
2 teaspoons gumbo filé (or to taste)
Salt and pepper, to taste

**Blue Ribbon**

★ ★ ★ ★ ★

*To make 1 cup of roux, combine ½ cup oil and ½ cup flour in a heavy skillet. Cook over medium heat, stirring constantly, until roux is caramel-color (about 20 minutes).*

**In a large pot,** bring the oyster water to a boil. Dissolve the roux in the boiling water, reduce the heat, and simmer for about 30 minutes. Add the onion, celery, pepper, and parsley. Bring to a boil, then reduce the heat and simmer for 30 minutes.

**Add** the hen (hen is used because the tougher meat stands up better than chicken to the long cooking time) and andouille. Simmer for 2 hours, or until the meat is tender. Add the oysters and boil for 15 minutes. Turn off the heat and add the gumbo filé and salt and pepper to taste. Serve over rice.

Rev. Msgr. J. Anthony Luminais, Bridge City, Louisiana
*Gumbo Festival, Bridge City, Louisiana*

# Creamy Crab Bisque

*6 servings*

   1 pound fresh crabmeat (preferably Maryland backfin crab)
   5 tablespoons butter
   ½ cup finely minced celery heart
   ¾ cup finely minced green onion
   2 tablespoons finely minced carrot
   1½ teaspoons finely minced garlic
   1 teaspoon ground ginger
   ¼ cup flour
   1¼ cups chicken broth
   1¼ cups whole milk
   2 pinches cayenne pepper
   2 pinches ground nutmeg
   ¼ teaspoon salt
   Pinch of white pepper
   ¼ teaspoon dried lemon peel
   1¼ cups light cream
   ¼ cup dry sherry

**Pick over** the crabmeat for cartilage and return to the refrigerator. Melt the butter in a 4-quart saucepan. Add the celery, green onion, carrot, garlic, and ginger. Cover and simmer over low heat until the vegetables are tender, about 4 to 5 minutes. Whisk in the flour. Gradually add the broth and milk, bringing the mixture to a boil while stirring constantly. Add the cayenne, nutmeg, salt, white pepper, lemon peel, cream, and sherry. Heat thoroughly. Stir in the crabmeat and cook until it is heated through. Do not boil. Serve immediately.

Lillian Flugrath, Columbia, Maryland
*National Hard Crab Derby, Crisfield, Maryland*

For kitchen tips and more recipes, go to www.almanac.com/food.

# Hungarian Garden Vegetable Chicken Soup

*15 servings*

3½- to 4½-pound whole chicken
6 cans (13¾ ounces each) chicken broth
1 large onion, chopped
1 bunch scallions, white and light green parts only, sliced
2 large carrots, thinly sliced
2 stalks celery, thinly sliced
4 or 5 parsnips, thinly sliced
1 medium zucchini, thinly sliced
1½ cups chopped green cabbage
2 medium tomatoes, peeled, seeded, and finely diced
¼ cup minced fresh parsley (or 2 tablespoons dried)
1 tablespoon minced fresh dill (or 1 teaspoon dried)
1 teaspoon freshly ground black pepper
1 tablespoon Hungarian paprika
1 cup uncooked fine egg noodles

**Place** the chicken in a large pot and pour the broth over it, adding water if necessary to cover the chicken completely. Cover the pot and bring to a boil. Lower the heat and simmer until the chicken is tender, about 1 hour. Remove the chicken from the pot and refrigerate it and the broth, preferably overnight.

**Skim** the top layer of fat off the broth. Remove the chicken from the bones, shred, and add to the broth. Add the onion, scallions, carrots, celery, parsnips, zucchini, cabbage, tomatoes, parsley, dill, pepper, and paprika. Bring to a boil, lower the heat, partially cover, and simmer until the vegetables are just tender, about 30 minutes. Add the noodles and cook until tender, about 5 minutes.

*Note: This soup freezes well.*

Julie DeMatteo, Clementon, New Jersey
*Recipe Contest Winner,* The Old Farmer's Almanac, *Dublin, New Hampshire*

# White Oyster Chili

*8 servings*

Alex DeSantis won first place and a $1,000 grand prize for this recipe. Although this recipe contains many ingredients, it is easy to prepare, and the judges called it "original and fantastic."

### Topping

1 cup fresh parsley
½ cup fresh cilantro
⅓ cup pine nuts, lightly toasted
⅓ cup freshly grated Parmesan cheese
3 cloves garlic, minced
2 or 3 jalapeño peppers, chopped
1 teaspoon fresh lime juice
⅔ teaspoon grated lime rind
⅔ cup olive oil

### Chili

1½ pints Maryland oysters
2 teaspoons olive oil
1 onion, chopped
2 cloves garlic, minced
2 cups fresh corn (or 1 package [10 ounces] frozen corn, thawed and drained)
1 can (4 ounces) diced green chilies with juice
1 teaspoon ground cumin
3 tablespoons fresh lime juice
4 to 6 drops Louisiana hot sauce
2 cups chicken broth or stock
4 cups cooked cannellini or white kidney beans (canned beans work fine)
Salt and freshly ground black pepper, to taste
½ to 1 cup crushed tortilla chips
½ to ⅔ cup shredded Monterey Jack cheese

**TIP**
*Blue Ribbon*

★ ★ ★ ★ ★

O*ysters are available live in the shell, fresh shucked, frozen, or canned. Shell oysters should be alive when you buy them. Look to see that the shells are tightly closed or close quickly when touched. Shucked oysters come in three sizes: counts, selects, and standards. Counts are the largest and are good for stews and entrées. Selects are smaller and perfect for frying and using as hors d'oeuvres. Standards are the smallest and are ideal for fritters.*

**To make the topping,** place the parsley, cilantro, pine nuts, Parmesan, and garlic in a food processor fitted with a metal blade. Process for 10 seconds. Add the jalapeños, lime juice, and lime rind and process for 10 to 15 seconds more. With the processor running, add the oil through the food chute and process just until well blended. Set aside.

**To make the chili,** drain the oysters, reserving the liquor. In a large saucepan, heat the oil. Sauté the onion and garlic until soft. Stir in the corn and cook for about 2 to 3 minutes. Add the chilies, cumin, lime juice, and hot sauce. Mix well. Add the broth, ½ cup of the reserved oyster liquor, and beans. Bring to a boil, lower the heat, and simmer for about 10 minutes. Add salt and pepper to taste. Add the oysters and cook at a high simmer (do not boil) until the edges begin to curl.

**Place** about 1 tablespoon each of crushed tortilla chips and cheese in individual soup bowls. Ladle the hot chili over the chips and cheese. Spoon some of the topping on each serving. Serve any remaining topping in a small bowl on the side.

Alex DeSantis Sr., East Windsor, New Jersey
*National Oyster Cook-off, St. Mary's Oyster Festival, Leonardtown, Maryland*

# St. Mary's Oyster Festival

## Leonardtown, Maryland

The St. Mary's Oyster Festival was started more than 35 years ago to raise money for charitable causes in southern Maryland and to promote the local seafood industry. The festival, which is held over a weekend in mid-October, attracts over 20,000 people. A highlight is the National Oyster Cook-off, which is promoted throughout the United States. In recent years, more than 300 recipes have been submitted and reviewed, with 12 finalists coming to Leonardtown to compete.

# Pumpkin Festival

## Morton, Illinois

For more than 35 years, Morton has been celebrating its status as "Pumpkin Capital of the World." The town, located 10 minutes southeast of Peoria, is the home of Nestle/Libby's pumpkin-packing plant. Each September, the harvest is celebrated with carnival rides, a banjo bash, punkin-chuckin' contests, footraces, arts and crafts, garden shows, and pumpkins of all sizes cooked in various ways. You can try pumpkin ice cream, pancakes, fudge, and chili. Butterfly pork chops and pumpkin pie are the specialties. About 40,000 people visited the three-day festival in 2003.

# Pumpkin Tortilla Soup

*12 servings*

1 broiler-fryer chicken
1 large onion, chopped
1 leek, washed and chopped
2 cans (28 ounces each) whole tomatoes, chopped
3 cups tomato juice
1 small bunch celery with heart, chopped
1 to 2 cups canned pumpkin
2 teaspoons chicken bouillon granules
2 cloves garlic, crushed
½ teaspoon freshly ground black pepper
Salt, to taste
6 corn tortillas
¼ cup fresh cilantro leaves for garnish
8 ounces Monterey Jack cheese, shredded, for garnish

**Place** the chicken in a large pot and cover with at least 1 gallon of water. Bring to a boil, then reduce the heat and simmer until very tender, about 1 hour. Remove the chicken from the bones and cut or tear into medium-size pieces; set aside.

**Strain** the broth and place in a clean pot. Add the onion, leek, tomatoes, tomato juice, celery, pumpkin, bouillon, and garlic. Simmer for about 1 hour. Add the chicken, pepper, and salt to taste and simmer for 15 minutes more.

**Preheat** the oven to 250° F. While the soup is in its final simmer, slice the tortillas into thin strips (a pizza cutter works well) and bake until crisp and golden brown. Pour the hot soup into bowls and garnish with the cilantro leaves, cheese, and tortilla strips.

Liz Deppe, Morton, Illinois
*Pumpkin Festival, Morton, Illinois*

# Garlic Mushroom Soup

*8 to 10 servings*

20 cloves garlic, peeled
1½ pounds fresh mushrooms, divided
4 tablespoons olive oil, divided
2 cups toasted bread crumbs
1 bunch fresh parsley, stems removed and
    finely chopped
10 cups fresh or canned chicken broth
Salt and pepper, to taste
Dash of Tabasco
Dry sherry (optional)

**In a food processor** or by hand, finely chop the garlic and 1 pound of the mushrooms. Cut the remaining ½ pound mushrooms into thin slices. In a 4-quart saucepan, heat 2 tablespoons of the oil and sauté the garlic and mushrooms for 3 minutes. Remove from the pan and set aside.

**Add** the remaining 2 tablespoons of oil to the pan and sauté the bread crumbs. Add the mushroom mixture to the crumbs, stir in the parsley, and sauté for 5 minutes. Add the broth and simmer, stirring frequently, for about 15 minutes. Season with salt and pepper to taste, Tabasco, and sherry to taste (if using).

J. O. Manis, Mill Valley, California
*Gilroy Garlic Festival, Gilroy, California*

**Blue Ribbon**

★ ★ ★ ★ ★

To peel off the papery skin of garlic quickly, press the clove firmly with the handle of a knife. Or place the cloves in very hot water for a couple of minutes before peeling. Store peeled cloves in vegetable or olive oil in a jar in the refrigerator. They won't dry out, and the oil will be flavored for use in salad dressings and stir-frying.

# GILROY GARLIC FESTIVAL

~

## Gilroy, California

The Gilroy Garlic Festival, held the last full weekend in July, calls itself the "world's best food festival." Gourmet food is the main attraction, but there is also live entertainment, competitions and races, and arts and crafts, all set in the lush rolling hills of California's Santa Clara Valley. The festival is sponsored by the Gilroy Garlic Festival Association, a nonprofit organization that uses the proceeds from the festival to support charitable groups and service organizations. From 1979 through 2003, the association contributed more than $6 million to charitable causes.

# Tried-and-True Beef Stew

*6 servings*

¼ cup flour
¼ teaspoon dried thyme
¼ teaspoon ground ginger
¼ teaspoon dried summer savory
2 to 3 pounds beef chuck, cut into 1½-inch cubes
2 tablespoons oil
1 tablespoon butter
1 large onion, thinly sliced
¾ cup dry red wine or water
1 quart beef stock (may be made with beef bouillon cubes)
2 or 3 bay leaves
Salt and pepper, to taste
6 small carrots
6 pearl onions
4 medium potatoes, peeled and quartered
5 ounces (½ package) frozen peas
3 tablespoons sour cream

**In a shallow dish,** combine the flour, thyme, ginger, and savory. Dredge the meat with 2 tablespoons of this mixture, shaking off any excess. Heat the oil and butter in a Dutch oven and brown the meat thoroughly. Remove the meat from the pan. Brown the onion until quite dark and crisp, but do not allow to burn. Remove from the pan. Pour the wine or water into the pan juices to deglaze the pan, then add the stock and bay leaves. Add salt and pepper to taste. Put the meat and onion back in the pan and simmer, covered, for 1½ to 2 hours, or until the meat is tender.

**About 30 minutes before the meat is done,** add the carrots, pearl onions, and potatoes. Add the peas during the last few minutes of cooking. Dissolve the remaining 2 tablespoons of the flour mixture in a little cold stock or water. Use it to thicken the gravy. Gradually whisk the sour cream into the thickened gravy, being careful not to allow it to boil.

Marion L. Brant, Punta Gorda, Florida
*Recipe Contest Winner,* The Old Farmer's Almanac, *Dublin, New Hampshire*

Chapter 3

Vegetables &
Side Dishes

# STOCKTON ASPARAGUS FESTIVAL

~

## Stockton, California

**E**very year during the last weekend in April, Stockton holds a two-day community-wide event honoring asparagus. Stockton, which is located in the San Joaquin–Sacramento Delta region, grows nearly 70 percent of the nation's fresh market asparagus. Festival activities include continuous asparagus-cooking demonstrations and a big-top tent called "asparagus alley," where gourmet asparagus dishes are prepared for festival-goers. Community projects benefit from the proceeds of the festival, which is sponsored by the City of Stockton.

A recipe contest is held before the festival. A committee selects 12 finalists, who meet in Stockton to prepare their entries. The grand prize winner is invited to demonstrate his or her recipe at the Asparagus Festival.

# San Joaquin Valley Enchiladas

*6 servings*

2 to 3 pounds fresh asparagus, cleaned and
    trimmed
½ cup oil
12 corn tortillas
½ cup (1 stick) butter
½ cup flour
¾ cup chicken broth
1 cup sour cream
½ cup green taco sauce
3 cups shredded Monterey Jack cheese, divided
3 cups shredded cooked white chicken meat
½ cup chopped onion
¼ cup freshly grated Parmesan cheese

**Blanch** and drain the asparagus. Cut into 1-inch pieces and set aside.

**Heat** the oil in a large skillet and cook each tortilla until soft. Set on paper towels to drain. In a small saucepan, melt the butter. Add the flour, stirring to blend. Add the broth and cook until thick and bubbly, stirring constantly. Add the sour cream and taco sauce. Heat thoroughly.

**Preheat** the oven to 425° F. Sprinkle each tortilla with 2 tablespoons Monterey Jack cheese, chicken, onion, and asparagus. Top with 3 tablespoons of the cream sauce. Roll up and place, seam side down, in a baking dish. Sprinkle the remaining cheese over the top. Cover with the Parmesan and remaining cream sauce. Bake for 25 minutes.

Liz Rotert, Stockton, California
*Stockton Asparagus Festival, Stockton, California*

### Blue Ribbon

★ ★ ★ ★ ★

*When selecting fresh asparagus, choose firm, straight stalks with a rich green color and closed, compact tips. It is a good idea to pick uniform stalks so that cooking time will be consistent.*

*For storage, trim the ends, wrap in damp paper towels, and seal in a plastic bag. When preparing asparagus, break or cut at the tender part of the stem and cook quickly in a small amount of water. If you're using asparagus in an appetizer or salad, plunge the cooked asparagus into ice water to stop the cooking process.*

# Stuffed Onion Rolls

*6 side-dish servings*

4 to 6 Vidalia onions
¼ cup (½ stick) butter, divided
1 tablespoon oil
⅓ cup minced Vidalia onion
1 pound ground chuck
½ cup plus 3 tablespoons dry bread crumbs
¼ cup milk
1 egg
Salt and pepper, to taste
1 tablespoon dried parsley

**Peel** the onions and place in a large pot. Cover with water and bring to a boil. Lower the heat and simmer until tender, about 40 minutes.

**While** the onions are cooking, prepare the stuffing. Heat 1 tablespoon of the butter and the oil in a skillet. Sauté the minced onion until limp and clear; do not brown. In a large bowl, combine the meat, minced onion, ½ cup of the bread crumbs, milk, egg, salt and pepper to taste, and parsley. Mix until well blended; set aside.

**When** the whole onions are cooked, remove from the water with a slotted spoon and drain on paper towels. When cool, strip off the large outer layers. Place 2 teaspoons of the meat mixture on the end of each onion strip and roll up. Continue until the meat mixture is gone.

**Preheat** the oven to 400° F. Melt the remaining 3 tablespoons butter in a baking dish to coat the bottom and sides. Turn each onion roll in the butter, coating all sides, and bake for 15 minutes. Sprinkle with the remaining 3 tablespoons bread crumbs. Bake for 15 minutes more.

Betty J. Carver, Warner Robins, Georgia
*Georgia National Fair, Perry, Georgia*

# Sweet Carrots and Green Grapes

*6 servings*

½ cup (1 stick) butter
4 cups peeled and julienned carrots
1 cup seedless green grapes cut in half
2 tablespoons honey
1 tablespoon fresh lemon juice
Pinch of salt
3 or 4 fresh mint leaves, finely chopped, for garnish

**Melt** the butter in a large skillet. Add the carrots and stir until well coated. Cover and cook until almost tender, about 10 minutes, stirring occasionally. Add the grapes, honey, and lemon juice. Cook on low heat for 5 minutes more. Add the salt and garnish with the mint.

Rae Ann Sheffield, Holtville, California
*Holtville Carrot Festival, Holtville, California*

## HOLTVILLE CARROT FESTIVAL

### Holtville, California

**M**ore than 50 years ago, Holtville declared itself the "Carrot Capital of the World." Every year in late January or early February, Holtville celebrates the local harvest with a week of fun— a banquet, golf tournament, carnival, parade, arts and crafts sale, and carrot cook-off. The cooking contest has many categories, so anyone can find a suitable slot to enter his or her creation.

# Spinach Festival

~

## Crystal City, Texas

D ale Barker, editor and publisher of the local newspaper, the *Zavala County Sentinel*, is Crystal City's unofficial spokesman for spinach. He is the son of a large spinach producer and enjoys perpetuating a good-natured rivalry between Crystal City and nearby Alma, Arkansas, for the title of "Spinach Capital." Both towns have statues of Popeye next to City Hall, and both have large spinach-processing plants and canneries.

Crystal City holds its annual Spinach Festival on the first weekend in November. The town was officially proclaimed the "Spinach Capital of the World" in 1936 by then–Texas Governor James V. Allred. Townspeople build giant spinach salads, wear spinach hats and T-shirts, and sample cook-off dishes from dips to quiche and even dessert.

# Crepes Filled with Spinach Vera Cruz

*12 crepes*

*Crepes*

1 cup flour
2 eggs
1¾ cups milk
½ teaspoon salt
1 tablespoon butter, melted

*Filling*

3 strips bacon
¼ cup chopped onion

1 cup cooked fresh or frozen
　　spinach, squeezed dry
2 medium tomatoes, peeled,
　　seeded, and chopped
1 cup sour cream
1 cup shredded Monterey Jack
　　cheese, divided
Dash of Tabasco
Salt and pepper, to taste

**To make the crepes,** combine the flour, eggs, milk, salt, and butter in a blender or food processor. Brush a 4- to 6-inch skillet or crepe pan with butter. Pour in about 1½ tablespoons of the batter and tilt the pan so that the batter covers the bottom. Cook quickly on both sides. Butter the pan before cooking each crepe. Set the crepes aside while preparing the filling.

**To make the filling,** cook the bacon in a large skillet. Remove the bacon from the pan, reserving the drippings, and drain. Crumble when cool. In about 2 tablespoons of bacon fat, sauté the onion until soft. Add the spinach, tomatoes, and crumbled bacon. Stir in the sour cream, ¾ cup of the cheese, Tabasco, and salt and pepper to taste. Mix thoroughly. Cook until the cheese is melted.

**Preheat** the oven to 350° F. Place about 2 tablespoons of spinach filling on each crepe, roll it up, and place, seam side down, in a buttered 9x13-inch baking dish. Put a little additional filling on top and sprinkle with the remaining ¼ cup cheese. Bake until bubbly, about 15 to 20 minutes.

Dale Barker, Crystal City, Texas
*Spinach Festival, Crystal City, Texas*

# Italian Gold

*12 squares*

8 strips lean bacon
1 medium onion, chopped
2 cloves garlic, chopped
1 pound fresh mushrooms, chopped
1 tablespoon chopped fresh chives
Freshly ground black pepper
4 tablespoons Italian-style bread crumbs, divided
2 sheets phyllo
1 tablespoon butter, melted
Whole fresh chives

*Blue Ribbon*

★ ★ ★ ★ ★

S tore mushrooms unwashed, covered with a damp paper towel, in a brown paper bag. Do not store in plastic wrap, or the mushrooms will become slimy. When cleaning mushrooms, do not immerse in water, because they will absorb the moisture. Just wipe them clean with a damp paper towel or cloth.

**Fry** the bacon in a large skillet and remove from the pan. When the bacon is cool, crumble and set aside. In the bacon drippings, sauté the onion and garlic until soft. Add the mushrooms and sauté until golden brown. Remove the pan from the heat. Add the bacon bits, chopped chives, pepper to taste, and 3 tablespoons of the bread crumbs.

**Lay** one sheet of phyllo on a cutting surface and brush lightly with the melted butter. Sprinkle with the remaining 1 tablespoon bread crumbs. Place another sheet of phyllo on top. With a sharp knife, cut into 12 equal squares. Divide the mushroom-bacon filling among the squares. Gather the corners of each square into a peak and twist gently.

**Preheat** the oven to 400° F. Drop long strands of chives into boiling water for 5 seconds. Tie one strand around the neck of each phyllo "purse," tying the ends into a bow. Transfer to a baking sheet and bake for about 12 minutes, or until golden.

Barbara C. Kroll, Kennett Square, Pennsylvania
*Mushroom Cook-off, Mushroom Festival, Kennett Square, Pennsylvania*

# MUSHROOM FESTIVAL

~

## Kennett Square, Pennsylvania

September is National Mushroom Month, and in Kennett Square, the "Mushroom Capital of the World," they hold a tribute to the delicate fungi. Located in the heart of the historic Brandywine Valley, Kennett Square draws thousands of tourists to the annual Mushroom Festival. There are free mushroom farm tours, a mushroom-picking contest (spectators get samples after judging), and, the high point, tasting the competing recipes. If you're confused about which mushrooms are which, head to the nearby Mushroom Museum at Phillips Place and see shiitakes, chanterelles, criminis, portabellas, buttons, oysters, and many other varieties.

# Savory Vidalia Onion Turnovers

*40 wontons*

1 package (8 ounces) cream cheese,
    softened
1½ cups finely chopped Vidalia onion
1 scallion, chopped
½ cup finely chopped fresh mushrooms
½ cup shredded Cheddar cheese
½ cup shredded crabmeat
40 wonton wrappers
Oil for deep-frying

**In a large bowl,** combine the cream cheese, onion, scallion, mushrooms, cheese, and crabmeat. Mix well. Spoon a heaping tablespoon of the mixture in the center of a wonton wrapper. Fold over one side, wetting the edges with water to seal. Bend the edges around. Deep-fry until golden brown.

Carla DeFore, Byron, Georgia
*Georgia National Fair, Perry, Georgia*

**TIP**

*Blue Ribbon*

★ ★ ★ ★ ★

*W*hen cutting an onion, control your tears by starting at the top. The sulfuric compounds that make you cry are concentrated in the root end. When you are using only half an onion, use the top half; the root end will stay fresher longer.

Chapter 4

Fish &
Seafood

# CHARLESTOWN SEAFOOD FESTIVAL

~

## Charlestown, Rhode Island

**A**lways held the first Sunday in August, the Charlestown Seafood Festival draws more than 40,000 people to Ninigret Park. There are arts and crafts booths, a rock wall, motorcycle and car shows, rides, and a chowder cook-off. You'll find lobsters, clam cakes, chowder, fish and chips, fish kebabs, and other treats to enjoy while at the festival.

# Seafood Lasagna

*12 servings*

1 pound curly lasagna noodles
½ cup (1 stick) butter
1 pound medium shrimp, shelled and deveined
1 pound scallops
⅓ cup white wine
3 cloves garlic, minced
2 lobsters, 1 pound each, boiled and shelled
1 container (16 ounces) ricotta cheese
1 egg
1½ teaspoons dried oregano
1½ teaspoons dried basil
1 pound Cheddar cheese, shredded
1 pound mozzarella cheese, shredded
½ cup bread crumbs

**Preheat** the oven to 350° F. Cook and drain the lasagna noodles. Melt the butter in a large skillet and sauté the shrimp and scallops. Add the wine and garlic and simmer for 5 minutes. Remove from the heat. Dice the lobster meat and add to the shrimp and scallops. Drain and set aside.

**In a large bowl,** combine the ricotta, egg, oregano, basil, and Cheddar. Mix thoroughly. Arrange a layer of noodles in a greased 9x14-inch baking dish. Layer half the ricotta mixture, half the seafood, and one-third of the mozzarella over the noodles. Repeat once. Top with the remaining noodles, mozzarella, and bread crumbs. Bake for 50 minutes.

Don Dubeau, West Warwick, Rhode Island
*Charlestown Seafood Festival, Charlestown, Rhode Island*

# Lily's Crab Cakes

*8 cakes*

For best results, use fresh crabmeat, squeezed dry. Canned crabmeat tends to be too moist for the desired texture.

1 pound fresh crabmeat
2 tablespoons dried parsley
1 slice hearty white bread, dried and crumbled
¼ teaspoon dried lemon peel
1 egg
1 egg yolk
3 tablespoons mayonnaise
2 teaspoons horseradish
2 teaspoons horseradish mustard
1 tablespoon Worcestershire sauce
5 drops Tabasco
⅛ teaspoon freshly ground black pepper
Vegetable oil for frying

**Pick over** the crabmeat for shells and cartilage. Put the crabmeat in a large bowl and add the parsley, bread crumbs, and lemon peel. Toss lightly. In a separate bowl or glass measuring cup, beat the egg and the egg yolk, using a wire whisk. Add the mayonnaise and beat until smooth. Add the horseradish, mustard, Worcestershire sauce, Tabasco, and pepper and beat until smooth.

**Pour** half the liquid over the crabmeat and toss lightly with a fork. Add the remaining liquid and toss lightly again. Gently pat the mixture into patties (about ⅓ cup each). Chill for 30 minutes.

**In a heavy skillet,** heat ¼ inch vegetable oil. When the oil is hot, fry the crab cakes over medium heat until golden brown on both sides, about 4 to 6 minutes per side. Drain on paper towels. Serve with Lily's Tartar Sauce (recipe follows).

# Lily's Tartar Sauce

*½ cup*

½ cup mayonnaise
2 tablespoons sweet relish
1 tablespoon capers, mashed
1½ teaspoons horseradish mustard
⅛ teaspoon grated lemon rind

**In a small bowl,** combine the mayonnaise, relish, capers, mustard, and lemon rind. Serve with Lily's Crab Cakes.

Lillian Flugrath, Columbia, Maryland
*National Hard Crab Derby, Crisfield, Maryland*

## NATIONAL HARD CRAB DERBY
### Crisfield, Maryland

The National Hard Crab Derby began in 1947, when a few hard crabs were dumped in a circle on Main Street and the crab that scurried to an outer circle first was declared the winner. Its owner received a trophy. Every year since its humble beginning, the National Hard Crab Derby has grown, and now activities span the Labor Day weekend. There are parades, boat-docking contests, a beauty pageant, a crab-picking contest, arts and crafts, fireworks, crab races, and a crab-cooking contest.

# KANSAS CITY
# BARBEQUE SOCIETY CONTEST

~

## Kansas City, Missouri

T he Kansas City Barbeque Society is the world's largest organization of barbecue enthusiasts. The society publishes a monthly newspaper, *The Bullsheet,* and sanctions more than 50 barbecue contests across the United States. It is a clearinghouse of information and publishes a great cookbook complete with a calendar of contests and a resource guide to barbecue sauces, seasonings, and spices (see Appendix).

# The Only Barbecued Salmon

*4 servings*

David Veljacic, a Vancouver fireman, has captured prizes internationally for his barbecued salmon recipe. David's cookbook, *The Fire Chef: Fast Grilling & Slow Cooking on the Barbecue* (Douglas & McIntyre, May 1999), was on the best-seller lists for almost two years, following publication.

**8 large cloves garlic, finely chopped**
**1 teaspoon salt**
**¼ cup finely chopped fresh parsley**
**2 tablespoons minced sun-dried tomatoes**
**¼ cup olive oil**
**1 large salmon fillet (1½ pounds), boned (preferably sockeye, coho, or spring salmon)**

**Sprinkle** the garlic and salt in a shallow dish. Mash the garlic with the blade of a knife. In a small bowl, combine the mashed garlic, parsley, tomatoes, and oil. Mix well. Cover and refrigerate for 8 hours or overnight.

**Prepare** the grill for cooking. Cut two lengthwise slits in the salmon fillet with a sharp knife, dividing the surface of the fish into thirds. (Cut to the skin but not through it.) Spread half the garlic mixture over the fillet and into the slits. Place the salmon, skin side down, on a greased grill rack. Cover the grill and cook over low heat for 10 to 15 minutes. Spread the remaining garlic mixture on the fish. Continue cooking, with the lid down, over medium heat for 15 minutes, or until the fish flakes easily. Remove from the grill by inserting spatulas between the skin and the flesh, lifting the fillet, and leaving the skin on the grill. Serve the skinless, boneless fillet on a bed of fresh greens.

Pat and David Veljacic, Coquitlam, British Columbia
*Kansas City Barbeque Society Contest,*
*Kansas City, Missouri*

**Blue Ribbon**

★ ★ ★ ★ ★

*When choosing fish, look for shiny skin that springs back when touched. The flesh should be firm and elastic, and the eyes should be bright and clear, not cloudy and sunken. If the fish has a strong odor, it is probably old or has not been stored properly. Fresh fish should be sold no more than two to three days out of the water.*

# Jim's Shrimp and Lobster Espanole

*4 servings*

6 ounces long-grain rice
6 ounces wild rice
2 tablespoons plus ¼ cup (½ stick) butter, divided
2 small onions, diced
1 green bell pepper, diced
½ pound fresh mushrooms, diced
3 tomatoes, peeled and halved
¾ pound lobster meat
1 pound Maine shrimp, cooked, peeled, and deveined
¼ cup sherry
1 teaspoon lemon juice
1 teaspoon Worcestershire sauce
Salt and pepper, to taste
1 tablespoon chopped fresh parsley for garnish

**Cook** the long-grain and wild rice according to the package directions; set aside. Melt the 2 tablespoons butter in a large skillet and sauté the onion, pepper, and mushrooms for 5 minutes. Add the tomatoes and simmer until the vegetables are tender but not mushy. Cut the lobster meat into bite-size pieces. Melt the remaining ¼ cup butter in another skillet. Sauté the lobster and shrimp for 2 minutes. Add the sherry, lemon juice, Worcestershire sauce, and salt and pepper to taste. Heat thoroughly. Arrange the rice on a heated serving platter. Top with the seafood, then the vegetable mixture. Garnish with the parsley.

James Povac, Camden, Maine
*Lobster Festival, Rockland, Maine*

# LOBSTER FESTIVAL

## Rockland, Maine

In 1947, the first annual Camden-Rockport Lobster Festival offered "all the lobster you can eat for $1," which caused the festival to lose money but not heart. It has continued for over 55 years with two main attractions — Maine lobster (the price has gone up some) and a big parade. Since 1950, King Neptune and his royal court have opened each festival by arriving from the sea, accompanied by the reigning sea goddess and characters such as Blackbeard, a sea hag, sea nymphs, lobsters, and mermaids. The festival, operated by the Rockland Festival Corp., is held in the beginning of August at the Rockland public landing. At the 2003 festival, a total of 25,000 pounds of lobster was served to a crowd of nearly 100,000 people.

# Crab Quesadillas

*6 servings*

1 pound lump crabmeat
1 tablespoon olive oil or vegetable oil
1 medium green bell pepper, cut into strips
½ medium red bell pepper, cut into strips
½ medium yellow bell pepper, cut into strips (optional)
1 medium onion, sliced into rings
1 clove garlic, minced
¼ cup chopped fresh cilantro
⅓ cup mayonnaise
¼ teaspoon cayenne pepper
⅛ teaspoon ground cumin
1½ cups shredded Cheddar cheese, divided
1½ cups shredded Monterey Jack cheese, divided
Juice of ½ lime
1 small jalapeño pepper, seeded and finely chopped
12 (6-inch) flour tortillas
Vegetable cooking spray
Lime slices, salsa, sour cream, and/or guacamole for garnish

**Preheat** the oven to 450° F. Check the crabmeat for pieces of shell and cartilage. In a large skillet, heat the oil over medium heat. Add the green, red, and yellow (if using) bell peppers, onion, and garlic. Cook for 5 to 10 minutes.

**In a large bowl,** combine the crabmeat, cilantro, mayonnaise, cayenne, cumin, 1 cup of the Cheddar, 1 cup of the Monterey Jack, lime juice, and jalapeño. Gently fold the ingredients together to avoid breaking the crabmeat.

**Place** six tortillas on large oiled baking sheets. Divide the pepper-onion mixture equally among the tortillas. Divide the crabmeat mixture equally among them. Sprinkle the remaining ½ cup Cheddar and the remaining ½ cup Monterey Jack on top and cover with the tortillas left in the package. Lightly spray the top of each tortilla with vegetable cooking spray. Bake for 7 to 10 minutes. Cut each tortilla into quarters and garnish with lime slices, salsa, sour cream, and/or guacamole.

John M. Pachkowski, Wilmington, Delaware
*National Hard Crab Derby, Crisfield, Maryland*

# Chapter 5

## Meat & Poultry

# STATE FAIR OF TEXAS

*Dallas, Texas*

The State Fair of Texas, founded in 1886, had as its earliest attractions horse races, cattle sales, balloon ascents, and farm machinery displays. It has grown to a 24-day showcase of entertainment, exhibits, and competitions presented each fall in Dallas. Millions of people attend, making it one of the largest annual expositions in the world. Highlights have included P. T. Barnum's most extraordinary acts and animals; free concerts by Wynona, the Beach Boys, and top country stars; an NBA jam session with special appearances by professional basketball players; a giant car show; a free-flight bird show with eagles, hawks, condors, and falcons; and nightly fireworks.

# Tex-Mex Fried Pies

*12 pies*

*Crust*

2 cups flour
½ teaspoon salt
1 cup shredded Cheddar cheese
⅔ cup shortening
5 to 6 tablespoons water

*Filling*

1 pound ground beef
1 medium onion, chopped
⅓ cup finely chopped red bell
    pepper

⅓ cup finely chopped green bell
    pepper
¼ cup picante sauce
½ cup finely crushed potato chips
1 package (1¼ ounces) taco
    seasoning mix
1 cup shredded Cheddar cheese
¼ teaspoon garlic powder (or 1
    clove garlic, finely chopped)
1 egg beaten with 1 tablespoon
    water
Oil for frying

**To make the crust,** place the flour, salt, and cheese in a food processor. Add the shortening and process for 15 seconds. Sprinkle the water through the food chute, 1 tablespoon at a time, just until a dough forms. Shape into a ball and divide in half. Chill for 30 minutes. Roll and cut into 4- to 5-inch circles.

**To make the filling,** put the ground beef in a large skillet and sauté until almost cooked. Add the onion and red and green bell peppers. Continue to cook until the meat is done and the onion is translucent. Stir in the picante sauce, potato chips, taco seasoning mix, cheese, and garlic powder. Cook until heated through. Let the mixture cool slightly before filling the pastries.

**Place** a little filling in the center of each pastry circle. Brush the edges of the dough with the egg-water mixture. Fold the dough over the filling, seal, and crimp with the tines of a fork. Heat ¼ inch oil in a large skillet and fry the pastries until lightly browned, about 2 minutes per side. Serve hot.

Robert E. Baker, Dallas, Texas
*State Fair of Texas, Dallas, Texas*

# World's Championship Chili Cook-Off

## International Chili Society

### San Juan Capistrano, California

The International Chili Society in San Juan Capistrano sponsors the World's Championship Chili Cook-off the first weekend in October. Here the winner receives $25,000. Nearly all the contestants prepare "real" chili—a mixture of beef, onion, garlic, chili powder, and cumin—based on the traditional Texas trail cook's specialty. (Beans were occasionally added to stretch the stew if there were too many cowboys to feed, but they are not considered authentic.)

The ICS is a nonprofit organization that sanctions cook-offs. These events are worldwide and benefit charities and nonprofit organizations. In 2000, over 300 chili cook-offs were held by the ICS, with over one million people tasting, cooking, judging, and having fun!

# Costa Mesa Chili

*6 servings*

You may substitute 7 tablespoons good-quality chili powder in place of the three specific types mentioned.

**2 cans (10½ ounces each) chicken broth, divided**
**½ cup tomato sauce**
**3 tablespoons pure California chili powder**
**1 tablespoon pure New Mexico chili powder**
**3 tablespoons Gebhardt chili powder**
**2 tablespoons ground cumin**
**1 teaspoon salt**
**3 teaspoons oil (approximately), divided**
**1 small onion, chopped**
**5 to 7 cloves garlic, minced**
**2½ pounds tri-tip or bottom sirloin, cut into ¼-inch cubes**
**    or coarsely ground**
**½ to 1 teaspoon Tabasco (to taste)**

**In a large pot,** combine 1½ cans of the broth, tomato sauce, chili powders, cumin, and 1 teaspoon salt. Bring to a boil, then reduce the heat to a simmer.

**Meanwhile,** in a large skillet, heat 1 teaspoon of the oil and sauté the onion and garlic over low heat until tender. Add to the sauce. In the same skillet, adding oil as needed, sauté the meat, one-third at a time, until no longer pink. Add to the sauce. Bring to a boil, reduce the heat, and simmer for 2½ hours, adding more chicken broth as needed. Thirty minutes before serving, add the Tabasco and salt to taste.

Norm Gaul, Costa Mesa, California
*World's Championship Chili Cook-off, International Chili Society,*
*San Juan Capistrano, California*

# BIG PIG JIG

## Vienna, Georgia

I n 2003, the Southeast's oldest and largest barbecue contest, the Big Pig Jig, drew 120 teams to Vienna to cook more than 400 entries of hog shoulders, ribs, Brunswick stew, and barbecue sauce for $12,000 in prize money. In the Big Pig Jig Village, you'll find 15 square blocks of barbecue shanties and team names such as Hot Shots, Sporty Porkers, and Meat Doctors. For those who aren't slaving over the smokers, there is a parade, local and national entertainment, carnival rides, arts and crafts, and a 5k "hog jog."

# Award-Winning Barbecued Ribs

*10 to 12 servings*

L & L Cooking Crew comprises a group of friends gathered together to enjoy the festivities at cooking festivals around the Southeast. They have won several state championships, including those in Georgia, South Carolina, and Tennessee.

½ cup plus 2 tablespoons paprika
¼ cup salt
¼ cup garlic powder
¼ cup chili powder
¼ cup plus 2 tablespoons brown sugar
Crushed red pepper
4 slabs pork loin back ribs (13 to 15 ribs per slab)

**In a medium bowl,** combine the paprika, salt, garlic powder, chili powder, brown sugar, and red pepper to taste. The team of cooks that devised this recipe says to taste this "dry rub" before applying it to the meat. You are checking for hotness or flatness. It is strong and should be used with a light hand.

**Start** a fire in the smoker, add water (and keep water in the pan), and let the temperature rise to about 225° F. Sprinkle the rub on the meaty side of the slabs. Place the meat in the smoker (bone side down, on the top rack), close the dome, and let the temperature come back to 225° F. Cook, checking every 45 minutes, for about 4 to 6 hours. The ribs are done when one end of the slab tears easily when bent back with a pair of tongs. A few minutes before serving, baste with a finishing sauce.

**If** you'd like to try this recipe on your grill at home, cut it in half. Keep in mind that real barbecue means meat cooked slowly by the smoke of a fire that is mostly coals. For those of you who don't have a home smoker and are using a grill, fire up about 30 briquettes. When they are about 80 percent ash, spread the coals and grill the ribs 6 inches above the hot coals for 1½ hours. Turn the meat every 15 to 20 minutes and baste with barbecue sauce.

L & L Cooking Crew, Larry Haynie, Chief Cook, Jonesboro, Georgia
*Big Pig Jig, Vienna, Georgia*

# Grecian Skillet Rib Eyes

*2 to 4 servings*

Fran Yuhas won the "Best of Beef" prize at the Idaho Beef Cook-off with this recipe, which can be prepared in 25 minutes and incorporates Mediterranean flavors. Along with top honors, she took home $25,000 and a pro-design kitchen range.

1½ teaspoons garlic powder
1½ teaspoons dried basil, crumbled
1½ teaspoons dried oregano, crumbled
½ teaspoon salt
⅛ teaspoon freshly ground black pepper
2 well-trimmed rib-eye steaks, 1 inch thick (about 1 pound)
1 tablespoon olive oil
1 tablespoon fresh lemon juice
2 tablespoons crumbled feta cheese
1 tablespoon chopped Kalamata or ripe olives

**In a small bowl,** combine the garlic powder, basil, oregano, salt, and pepper. Press into both sides of the steaks. In a large nonstick skillet, heat the oil over medium heat. Place the steaks in the skillet and cook for about 10 to 14 minutes for medium-rare to medium doneness, turning once. Sprinkle with the lemon juice. Sprinkle the cheese and olives over the steaks and serve.

Fran Yuhas, Scotrun, Pennsylvania
*Idaho Beef Cook-off, Boise, Idaho*

# Death Row Bourbon Sauce

*3½ cups*

2 tablespoons vegetable oil
½ cup finely chopped onion
1 clove garlic, minced
2 cups ketchup
½ cup bourbon whiskey, divided
¼ cup raspberry vinegar
¼ cup Worcestershire sauce
3 tablespoons molasses
2 tablespoons prepared mustard
2 tablespoons soy sauce
2 tablespoons hot sauce or 1 tablespoon
    Tabasco
½ teaspoon coarsely ground black pepper
¼ teaspoon cayenne pepper
¼ teaspoon liquid smoke (optional)

**In a medium saucepan,** heat the oil over medium heat. Add the onion and garlic and sauté until tender, about 5 minutes. Add the ketchup, ¼ cup of the whiskey, vinegar, Worcestershire sauce, molasses, mustard, soy sauce, hot sauce or Tabasco, black pepper, and cayenne. Mix thoroughly. Cook for 2 hours in the smoker or add the liquid smoke and simmer for 20 minutes over low heat on the stovetop. Stir in the remaining ¼ cup whiskey. Use as a baste or a finishing and table sauce on pork, beef, and chicken. This sauce also is good in baked beans. It will keep for several weeks in the refrigerator.

Barbara Correll, Washington, D.C.
*Jack Daniel's Cook-off, Lynchburg, Tennessee*

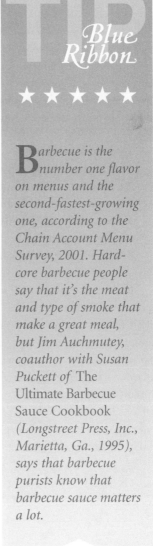

TIP

*Blue Ribbon*

★ ★ ★ ★ ★

**B**arbecue is the number one flavor on menus and the second-fastest-growing one, according to the Chain Account Menu Survey, 2001. Hardcore barbecue people say that it's the meat and type of smoke that make a great meal, but Jim Auchmutey, coauthor with Susan Puckett of The Ultimate Barbecue Sauce Cookbook (Longstreet Press, Inc., Marietta, Ga., 1995), says that barbecue purists know that barbecue sauce matters a lot.

# Baked Apples Filled with Sausage

*6 servings*

Morris Shanstrom has loved cooking since he was a boy. During the Depression, his family took in a woman who cooked and cleaned for them, and she taught Morris to bake bread and cinnamon rolls. To this day, he bakes for his family every week. He and his wife taught cooking in 4-H, and they and their two children have given cooking demonstrations on television. His daughter surprised him by entering him in his first cooking contest, a Jimmy Dean sausage cook-off, and he won. When Morris retired over 20 years ago, he enrolled in culinary school. He thinks of cooking as an activity the whole family can do together.

**1 pound bulk sausage**
**6 large tart baking apples**
**2 tablespoons brown sugar**
**1 teaspoon ground cinnamon**
**¼ teaspoon grated lemon rind**
**¼ cup chopped figs**
**Brown sugar, ground cinnamon, grated lemon rind, or chopped figs**

**Preheat** the oven to 375° F. Brown the sausage in a large skillet. Wash the apples and cut a slice from the tops. Scoop out the flesh, leaving shells ½ inch thick. Cut the flesh from the cores and chop it. Add the chopped apple, brown sugar, cinnamon, lemon rind, and figs to the sausage and mix well. Fill the apple shells with the mixture. Sprinkle the tops with brown sugar, cinnamon, grated lemon rind, or chopped figs. Place in a baking dish, cover, and bake until tender, about 40 minutes. Serve with hot biscuits and a green salad.

Morris Shanstrom, Pueblo, Colorado
*Colorado State Fair and Exposition, Pueblo, Colorado*

For kitchen tips and more recipes, go to www.almanac.com/food.

# Olympic Seoul Chicken

*4 servings*

¼ cup white vinegar
3 tablespoons soy sauce
2 tablespoons honey
¼ teaspoon ground ginger
3 tablespoons peanut oil
8 broiler-fryer chicken thighs, skinned
10 cloves garlic, coarsely chopped
1 teaspoon crushed red pepper

**In a small bowl,** mix together the vinegar, soy sauce, honey, and ginger; set aside. In a large frying pan, heat the oil to a medium-high temperature. Add the chicken and cook, turning often, for about 10 minutes, or until browned on all sides. Add the garlic and red pepper. Cook, stirring well, for 2 to 3 minutes. Add the vinegar mixture, cover, and cook for about 15 minutes, or until the chicken is fork-tender. Uncover and cook for a few minutes more, or until the sauce is slightly thickened. Serve with rice.

Muriel Brody, Cumberland, Rhode Island
*Delmarva Chicken Cooking Contest, Delmarva Chicken Festival,*
*Georgetown, Delaware*

# DELMARVA CHICKEN FESTIVAL

~

## Georgetown, Delaware

According to Delmarva festival organizers, Muriel Brody's recipe is an all-time favorite. The Delmarva Chicken Festival is held on a weekend in June on the Delmarva Peninsula of Delaware, Maryland, and Virginia. Here cooks tend a 10-foot frying pan with garden rakes, cooking up to 800 chicken quarters at a time. Children enjoy the egg toss, egg obstacle course, and sifting through a mountain of cornmeal for money. Entertainment includes bluegrass and country music, carnival rides, and arts and crafts.

# Stuffed Chicken with Apple Glaze

*4 to 6 servings*

1 broiler-fryer chicken
½ teaspoon salt
¼ teaspoon freshly ground black pepper
2 tablespoons oil
1 package (6 ounces) stuffing mix
1 cup grated apple
½ teaspoon grated lemon rind
¼ cup chopped walnuts
¼ cup raisins
¼ cup finely chopped celery
½ cup apple jelly
1 tablespoon lemon juice
½ teaspoon ground cinnamon

**Preheat** the oven to 350° F. Sprinkle the chicken cavity with the salt and pepper. Rub the outside of the chicken with the oil.

**In a large bowl,** prepare the stuffing according to the package directions. Add the apple, lemon rind, walnuts, raisins, and celery, mixing well. Stuff the chicken and place on a rack in a baking pan. Cover loosely with foil and roast for 25 minutes per pound (a little under 2 hours for a stuffed 4-pound bird). Place any extra stuffing in a covered casserole and bake for 1 hour.

**In a small saucepan,** combine the apple jelly, lemon juice, and cinnamon. Bring to a boil, then lower the heat and simmer for 3 minutes, stirring to prevent scorching. After 1 hour of roasting the chicken, remove the foil and brush with the glaze. Continue roasting, brushing frequently with glaze, for about 30 minutes more. The chicken is done when the leg moves freely when lifted and the internal temperature registers 180° F on a meat thermometer.

Ruth Dykes, Beltsville, Maryland
*Delmarva Chicken Cooking Contest, Delmarva Chicken Festival,*
*Georgetown, Delaware*

# Caribbean Chicken Drums

*4 servings*

2 tablespoons oil
8 chicken drumsticks
1 can (14½ ounces) whole peeled tomatoes, cut into chunks
1 can (4 ounces) diced green chilies
1 tablespoon brown sugar
¼ teaspoon ground allspice
¼ cup mango chutney, finely chopped
1 tablespoon fresh lemon juice
¼ cup dark seedless raisins
1 large banana, sliced
1 ripe mango, sliced, for garnish

**In a large skillet,** heat the oil to a medium temperature. Add the drumsticks and cook, turning often, for about 10 minutes, or until browned on all sides. Add the tomatoes, chilies, brown sugar, and allspice. Bring to a boil, cover, reduce the heat to low, and cook for 20 minutes. Add the chutney, lemon juice, and raisins. Cover and cook on low for about 15 minutes more, or until a fork can be inserted into the chicken with ease. Remove the chicken to a serving platter.

**Skim** the fat off the sauce. Add the banana and heat thoroughly. Spoon the fruit and a little sauce over the chicken. Garnish with mango slices. Place the remaining sauce in a separate dish and serve warm with the chicken.

Rosemarie Berger, Jamestown, North Carolina
*Grand Prize, National Chicken Cooking Contest, Washington, D.C.*

For kitchen tips and more recipes, go to www.almanac.com/food.

# NATIONAL CHICKEN COOKING CONTEST

~

Washington, D.C.

The National Chicken Cooking Contest is a premier competitive chicken cooking event. It was held annually from 1949–1983. The cook-off is now held every two years. One finalist from each state and the District of Columbia is chosen by a group of food specialists to cook his or her chicken dish at the national cook-off. The 51 finalists receive an all-expenses-paid trip to the competition. A different panel of nationally known food experts selects the top five winners, who share $36,000 in prize money.

# Southwestern Oven-Fried Chicken

*4 servings*

3 slices white bread, torn into small pieces
3 tablespoons fresh cilantro
2 tablespoons yellow cornmeal
2 tablespoons pine nuts
2 large cloves garlic, peeled
1½ teaspoons ground cumin
½ teaspoon dried oregano, crumbled
½ teaspoon salt, divided
¼ teaspoon cayenne pepper
⅛ teaspoon ground cloves
2 teaspoons egg white
2 tablespoons Dijon-style mustard
1 tablespoon water
2 teaspoons honey
4 broiler-fryer chicken drumsticks, skinned
4 broiler-fryer chicken thighs, skinned
¼ teaspoon freshly ground black pepper

**Place** the bread, cilantro, cornmeal, pine nuts, garlic, cumin, oregano, ¼ teaspoon of the salt, cayenne, and cloves in a food processor. Process to form fine crumbs. Add the egg white and mix until moist. Put the mixture in a large, shallow dish and set aside.

**Preheat** the oven to 400° F. In a small bowl, mix together the mustard, water, and honey. Brush over the chicken drumsticks and thighs. Sprinkle with the pepper and remaining ¼ teaspoon salt. Dredge the chicken with the bread crumbs, pressing gently so that a thin coating adheres. Place on a rack in a baking pan. Bake for about 40 minutes, or until the chicken is crisp and brown.

Judith Markiewicz, Canton, Ohio
*Grand Prize, National Chicken Cooking Contest, Washington, D.C.*

　　For kitchen tips and more recipes, go to www.almanac.com/food.

# Chapter 6

## Potatoes, Pasta, & Rice

# Dutch Oven Cook-off
## Idaho Spud Day
### Shelley, Idaho

For 75 years, the small town of Shelley has been celebrating Idaho's potato harvest. On the third Saturday in September, 10,000 people gather to eat free baked potatoes, watch potato-picking and -peeling contests, and enjoy a parade and talent show. Where else but at Spud Day can you see teams playing tug-of-war over a huge pit of mashed potatoes? In 1992, a team of speedy peelers set the Guinness World Record by peeling 1,064 pounds, 4 ounces of Idaho russets.

The highlight of the day is the Dutch Oven Cook-off, where six teams of chefs cook over hot coals in camp ovens. These cooks say that Dutch oven cooking is easy. The rule of thumb is that each charcoal briquette is worth about 25 degrees of heat, so you can adapt almost any recipe. When the coals have burned down to a white color, you place a specified number of briquettes under the pot and on the flat (not domed) lid.

# Dick's Original Dutch Oven Potatoes

*25 servings*

Dick Gardner is a caterer who specializes in outdoor cooking, and these Dutch oven potatoes are a mainstay of his menus. He even uses the Dutch oven for rolls, cakes, and scones. When baking in a Dutch oven, Dick maintains an even temperature of 350° F by using five briquettes beneath the oven and 15 to 18 on the lid. Dick believes that the winning taste in Dutch oven cooking comes from the fact that moisture is held in the heavy iron pot and the heat is dispersed more evenly, allowing for greater melding of flavors.

1 pound hot Italian sausage, cut into pieces
2 large onions, chopped
1 red bell pepper, chopped
1 green bell pepper, chopped
6 to 7 pounds Idaho potatoes, peeled and sliced
Pinch of freshly ground sage
Seasoned salt and freshly ground black pepper, to taste
1 pound sharp Cheddar cheese, shredded

**Build** a fire in your grill and let it burn to a bed of coals (about 30 minutes). Dick prefers a wood fire, but this recipe will work well with charcoal or gas.

**Place** the sausage in a 14-inch Dutch oven and put it on the coals to brown. Remove from the coals and add the onion and red and green bell peppers. Mix well. Add the potatoes and stir again. Pour in enough water so that you can see the potatoes sitting in it but they are not covered (about 1 quart). Sprinkle the sage over the top and cover. Place the Dutch oven back on the coals and cook until the potatoes are tender, adding more water if needed. Check every 2 to 5 minutes to make sure the potatoes don't burn. If you are using a wood fire, cooking time will be about 45 minutes. Charcoal will take a bit longer. Gas will take about 1 hour, but the potatoes will require closer watching.

**When the potatoes are cooked,** add seasoned salt and pepper to taste. Sprinkle the cheese on top and replace the lid, cooking just until the cheese is melted. Stir and serve.

Dick Gardner, Ucon, Idaho
*Dutch Oven Cook-off, Idaho Spud Day, Shelley, Idaho*

# Idaho Potato Fajitas

*4 servings*

Larry Mitchell won $1,000 for this recipe, which originated when he was making dinner for his children, ran out of tortilla shells, and had to make do. (Necessity is the father of invention.)

> 4 medium potatoes, scrubbed
> 1 jalapeño pepper, seeded and chopped
> ½ cup chicken broth
> 3 tablespoons oil, divided
> 1 red bell pepper, seeded and cut into ¼-inch chunks
> 1 sweet Spanish onion, sliced vertically
> 2 whole boneless, skinless chicken breasts, thinly sliced
> Chopped scallions and chopped fresh cilantro for garnish
> Salsa

**Place** the potatoes in a stovetop steamer or in the oven and cook until tender, about 45 to 55 minutes. In a blender, purée the jalapeño and broth; set aside. Heat 1 tablespoon of the oil in a large skillet and add the red pepper. Cook for 1 minute, stirring constantly. Remove the pepper with a slotted spoon and set aside. Add 1 tablespoon of the oil and sauté the onion for 30 seconds, stirring constantly. Remove and add to the pepper. Place the remaining 1 tablespoon of oil in the pan and add the chicken. Stir-fry for about 2 minutes. Add the jalapeño purée and cook for 2 minutes more. Add the pepper and onion and cook for 1 minute more, or until the chicken is thoroughly done.

**Place** the cooked potatoes on a serving plate, slash the tops, and squeeze open. Spoon the fajita mixture on the potatoes, garnish with the scallions and cilantro, and serve the salsa on the side.

Larry Mitchell, Caldwell, Idaho
*Idaho Original Cooking Contest, Idaho Spud Day, Shelley, Idaho*

# Potato Pizza

*10 to 12 servings*

**3 pounds potatoes, peeled and coarsely grated**
**½ teaspoon salt**
**3 eggs**
**1 medium onion, grated**
**8 strips bacon, cooked, drippings reserved**
**1 bunch broccoli, cut into florets**
**2 teaspoons butter**
**1 large onion, halved and thinly sliced**
**1 tablespoon chopped garlic**
**¼ cup chopped red bell pepper**
**2 cups sliced fresh mushrooms**
**1 cup ricotta cheese**
**3 cups shredded extra-sharp Cheddar cheese, divided**
**½ teaspoon dried oregano**
**Paprika**

**Place** the potatoes in a colander and toss with the salt. Let drain for 5 minutes, then press out any excess water. In a large bowl, lightly beat the eggs. Stir in the potatoes and grated onion. Press this mixture into an oiled 12-inch Dutch oven. Cook over 8 to 10 coals with 12 to 15 coals on the lid for 30 minutes. Remove the lid and brush the crust with the reserved bacon drippings. Cover and bake for 10 to 15 minutes more.

**Meanwhile,** blanch the broccoli for 1 minute, rinse with cold water, and set aside. Melt the butter in a large skillet. Add the sliced onion and garlic and sauté for 2 minutes. Add the pepper and mushrooms. Cook for 5 minutes more, or until the mushrooms have given off their liquid. Toss the vegetables with the broccoli.

**In a small bowl,** combine the ricotta, 2 cups of the Cheddar, and oregano. Spread on the baked crust, cover with the vegetables, and sprinkle with the remaining 1 cup Cheddar. Crumble the bacon on top and sprinkle with paprika. Cover the Dutch oven, return to the coals, and bake over 6 to 8 coals with 16 coals on the lid for 15 minutes.

Frank and Shelley Johnson, Rexburg, Idaho
*Dutch Oven Cook-off, Idaho Spud Day, Shelley, Idaho*

# Pudgeless Pumpkin Potatoes

*12 servings*

10 medium potatoes, peeled, boiled, and mashed
1 can (15 ounces) solid-pack pumpkin
1 package (8 ounces) cream cheese
½ cup fat-free sour cream
¼ cup (½ stick) light margarine
1 to 2 teaspoons garlic powder
1 teaspoon salt
Pinch of paprika
Pinch of dill weed

**Preheat** the oven to 350° F. In a large bowl, combine the potatoes, pumpkin, cream cheese, sour cream, margarine, garlic powder, and salt. Place in a 9x9-inch baking dish, sprinkle with the paprika and dill weed, and bake for 30 minutes. This recipe contains approximately 6 grams of fat per serving, compared to 10 grams per serving for the traditional version.

Peggy McFeeters, Morton, Illinois
*Pumpkin Festival, Morton, Illinois*

For kitchen tips and more recipes, go to www.almanac.com/food.

# Rob and Lee's Three-Garlic Pasta

*4 servings*

1 whole chicken breast
2 large heads garlic, divided
1½ tablespoons olive oil
1½ tablespoons butter
¼ cup chopped red onion
1 large tomato, peeled, seeded, and chopped
¼ teaspoon dried thyme
⅛ teaspoon white pepper
Salt and freshly ground black pepper, to taste
¼ cup dry white wine
¼ cup chicken stock
½ cup heavy cream
8 to 12 ounces cooked pasta (linguine or spaghetti)
2 tablespoons chopped fresh parsley for garnish

**In a smoker,** using hickory chips, smoke the chicken breast and 1 head of the garlic for 2 to 3 hours. If you do not have a smoker, substitute already-smoked chicken and roast 1 head of garlic in the oven. To roast the garlic, peel off the outer skin, leaving the cloves and head intact. Place the head on a double thickness of aluminum foil and brush with 1 teaspoon olive oil. Seal the foil and bake at 375° F for 45 to 55 minutes.

**Remove** the cloves from the other head of garlic. Finely chop 8 cloves and set aside. Then finely chop 3 more cloves (or to taste) and set aside. Heat the oil and butter in a cast-iron skillet. Add the 8 chopped garlic cloves and red onion and sauté until golden. Shred the smoked chicken and add to the skillet. If you are using bought smoked chicken instead of cooking your own with garlic, add the roasted garlic to the chicken-onion mixture by squeezing the garlic from the inner skins. Discard the skins. Add the tomato, thyme, white pepper, and salt and black pepper to taste. Mix well. Add the wine and stock and cook over medium heat for 5 minutes. Add the cream and cook over low heat for 8 minutes more. Add the remaining 3 chopped garlic cloves. Pour over the pasta and garnish with the parsley.

Rob Krol and Lee Ohanian, Northridge, California
*Gilroy Garlic Festival, Gilroy, California*

# Brown Onion Rice Casserole

*6 servings*

1 can (4 ounces) mushroom pieces with liquid (or ½ cup
    sliced fresh mushrooms)
⅓ cup butter, melted
1 cup white rice
1 cup chopped Vidalia onion
½ cup chopped green bell pepper
1 can (11 ounces) beef consommé plus ½ can water
Freshly ground black pepper
Pinch of garlic powder
3 to 4 drops Tabasco

**To prepare in the microwave,** place all the ingredients in a microwave-safe bowl and cook for 20 minutes. Stir and cook for 15 minutes more, or until the rice is done and all the liquid is absorbed.

**To prepare on the stovetop,** if you're using fresh mushrooms, sauté in the butter for 5 minutes. Place all the ingredients in a saucepan and cover. Bring to a boil and reduce the heat to a simmer. Cook until all the liquid is absorbed, about 30 minutes.

Ulma Lee Anderson, Reidsville, Georgia
*Vidalia Onion Festival, Vidalia, Georgia*

For kitchen tips and more recipes, go to www.almanac.com/food.

# Vidalia Onion Festival

~

Vidalia, Georgia

In 1931, farmer Moses Coleman planted some onions in Vidalia that proved unexpectedly sweet. Word of these treasures spread, and both production of and demand for the Vidalia Sweets grew. Farmers sought to preserve the uniqueness of their crop by acquiring what would amount to a legal patent on the onions. In 1986, Georgia's state legislature limited the growing area to 20 Georgia counties. Today in southeastern Georgia, warm spring breezes carry the aroma of newly harvested Vidalia onions to folks throughout this famous onion-growing region, letting them know that it's time to prepare for the annual onion festival. Vidalia has hosted the festival for 27 years, and it just keeps getting bigger and better. Each spring, in April or May, approximately 60,000 visitors come to enjoy a parade, the Miss Onion Pageant, softball and tennis tournaments, an onion run, arts and crafts, an air show, and an onion cook-off.

# Mexicali Wild Rice Casserole

*4 servings*

2 cups cooked wild rice
1 can (17 ounces) whole-kernel corn, drained (or about 2 cups frozen corn)
1 can (4 ounces) green chilies, drained and diced
2 cups mild chunky salsa or picante sauce
1 cup shredded Monterey Jack cheese

**Preheat** the oven to 350° F. In a medium bowl, combine the rice, corn, and chilies. Spread in a lightly oiled 7x11-inch baking dish. Pour the salsa or picante sauce over the rice and sprinkle with the cheese. Cover and bake for about 30 minutes, or until bubbly. Uncover and bake for 5 minutes more to brown.

Beth Anderson, Minneapolis, Minnesota
*Kelliher-Waskish Wild Rice Festival, Kelliher, Minnesota*

## KELLIHER-WASKISH WILD RICE FESTIVAL

### Kelliher, Minnesota

Kelliher and Waskish produce more than 3 million pounds of wild rice annually. For more than 25 years, the second weekend of July marked their annual celebration of wild rice, a nutty grain that locals call the "caviar of grains." (Wild rice is the only cereal grain native to North America.) Festival highlights included a wild rice pancake breakfast, food show, recipe contest, and parade, along with the Minnesota Wild Rice Queen Pageant. In the late 1990s, the Kelliher-Waskish Wild Rice Festival was replaced with the Kelliher Heritage Days Festival, which continues to celebrate the area's agricultural history.

# Chapter 7

## Quick & Yeast Breads

# CRANBERRY HARVEST FESTIVAL

## Carver, Massachusetts

Cranberries are the number one food crop in Massachusetts, with more than 500 growers producing more than 42 percent of the world's supply. Cranberries are one of only a few native North American fruits. They thrive in the special soil and water conditions found in wetlands. The bogs of Massachusetts evolved naturally from glacial deposits, which left impermeable kettle holes lined with clay. These beds filled with water and decaying matter, providing an ideal environment for cranberries.

Today the Cape Cod Cranberry Growers Association (CCCGA) helps farmers share new techniques, funds research, and promotes cranberry products and education. Together with Cranberry World, Ocean Spray's visitors center, the CCCGA sponsors the Cranberry Harvest Festival every October. Formerly held at the Edaville Cranberry Bog in Carver, the festival is now held in Plymouth. You can see cranberries harvested and screened, try all sorts of cranberry treats, and enjoy a craft fair, hayride, and farmer's market.

# Cranberry Applesauce Bread

*1 large loaf or 2 small loaves*

2 cups fresh or frozen cranberries, chopped
1 tablespoon plus ⅔ cup sugar, divided
½ cup (1 stick) butter, softened
1 egg
1 teaspoon vanilla extract
2 cups flour
1 teaspoon baking powder
1 teaspoon baking soda
1 teaspoon ground cinnamon
½ teaspoon salt
½ teaspoon ground nutmeg
1 cup applesauce
¼ cup milk
1 cup walnuts, chopped

**Preheat** the oven to 350° F. In a small bowl, toss the cranberries with the 1 tablespoon sugar and set aside. In a large bowl, cream the butter and remaining ⅔ cup sugar. Beat in the egg and vanilla. In another bowl, stir together the flour, baking powder, baking soda, cinnamon, salt, and nutmeg. In a separate bowl, combine the applesauce and milk. Add the flour mixture and the applesauce mixture alternately to the creamed mixture. Beat well. Stir in the cranberries and walnuts. Pour into one large or two small greased loaf pans. Bake for 50 minutes, or until a toothpick inserted in the center comes out clean. Remove to a wire rack and let cool before slicing.

Derolyn St. Louis, Freetown, Massachusetts
*Cranberry Harvest Festival, Carver, Massachusetts*

# Lemon Blueberry Tea Bread

*1 loaf*

1 cup fresh or frozen blueberries
1 tablespoon plus 1⅔ cups flour, divided
½ cup (1 stick) butter, softened
1½ cups sugar, divided
2 eggs
1½ teaspoons baking powder
¼ teaspoon salt
½ cup milk
1 tablespoon plus ¼ cup fresh lemon juice,
    divided
1 tablespoon grated lemon rind

**Preheat** the oven to 350° F. Toss the blueberries with the 1 tablespoon flour and set aside. In a large bowl, cream the butter with 1 cup of the sugar until fluffy. Add the eggs one at a time, beating well after each addition. In a separate bowl, combine the remaining 1⅔ cups flour, baking powder, and salt. Add the flour mixture and the milk alternately to the creamed mixture. Fold in the blueberries, 1 tablespoon lemon juice, and lemon rind. Pour into a greased and floured 9x5-inch loaf pan. Bake for about 1 hour, or until a knife inserted in the center comes out clean. Cool in the pan for 10 minutes before removing to a wire rack.

**In a small pan,** combine the remaining ½ cup sugar and the remaining ¼ cup lemon juice. Heat until boiling, stirring until the sugar dissolves. Brush on the slightly cooled bread and cool completely before cutting.

Karen Jean Kotick, Austintown, Ohio
*Canfield Fair, Canfield, Ohio*

**Blue Ribbon**

★ ★ ★ ★ ★

Always store bread at room temperature or in the freezer, not in the refrigerator. Refrigerated bread can go stale in as little as a day. Bread goes stale most rapidly at temperatures just above freezing. A deep, chest-type or commercial freezer has more stable temperatures than a small refrigerator freezer. To protect baked goods from freezer burn, wrap well in plastic wrap, then aluminum foil, then a zipper-locked bag with the air squeezed out.

# Chocolate Blueberry Muffins

*1 dozen muffins*

½ cup (1 stick) butter
3 squares (3 ounces) unsweetened chocolate
1 cup sugar
1 egg, slightly beaten
1 cup buttermilk
2 teaspoons vanilla extract
2 cups flour
1 teaspoon baking soda
1 cup fresh blueberries
2 squares (2 ounces) semisweet chocolate, melted

**Preheat** the oven to 375° F. In a medium saucepan, melt the butter and unsweetened chocolate over medium heat until smooth. Remove from the heat and cool slightly. Stir in the sugar, egg, buttermilk, and vanilla. In a small bowl, combine the flour and baking soda. Gently mix with the liquid ingredients. Fold in the blueberries. Spoon the batter into well-greased muffin cups, filling to the top. Bake for 25 to 30 minutes, or until a toothpick inserted in the center comes out clean. Transfer the muffins to a wire rack to cool. Drizzle the cooled muffins with the semisweet chocolate.

Kathy Rohrer, Puyallup, Washington
*Western Washington Fair, Puyallup, Washington*

# Maple Pecan Twists

*15 twists*

Alan Reid took top prize at the Michigan State Fair and Exposition for his Maple Pecan Twists. The recipe was later judged the best in a competition with more than 1,000 entries at the National Land O'Lakes Bake-off. He won $500 and a year's supply of Land O'Lakes dairy products.

*Filling*
- 1⅓ cups finely chopped pecans
- ¼ cup maple syrup
- 3 tablespoons brown sugar
- 1 teaspoon ground cinnamon

- 1 cup regular, light, or nonfat sour cream
- ¼ cup milk
- 1 egg
- 1 tablespoon butter, melted

*Dough*
- 2¾ cups plus 2 to 3 tablespoons flour
- 2 tablespoons sugar
- 1 teaspoon baking soda
- ½ teaspoon salt
- ½ cup (1 stick) butter, cut into pieces

*Glaze*
- 1 cup confectioners' sugar
- 1 tablespoon maple syrup
- 3 to 4 teaspoons milk

**Grease** two baking sheets. Preheat the oven to 400° F.

**To make the filling,** in a small bowl, combine the pecans, maple syrup, brown sugar, and cinnamon. Mix well and set aside.

**To make the dough,** in a large bowl, combine the 2¾ cups flour, sugar, baking soda, and salt. Cut in the butter pieces until the mixture is crumbly. In a medium bowl, combine the sour cream, milk, and egg. Beat with a wire whisk until smooth. Stir into the flour mixture just until a dough forms. Sprinkle your work surface with the remaining 2 to 3 tablespoons flour.

**Turn** the dough out onto the floured surface and knead 12 to 15 times. Roll the dough into a 15x12-inch rectangle. Brush with the melted butter. Sprinkle the filling over half the dough along the long edge. Fold the dough over the filling. Cut into 15 one-inch strips. Twist the strips about three times and place them on the baking sheets, pressing the ends onto the sheets.

**Bake** for 10 to 12 minutes, or until golden brown. Remove from the oven and transfer to wire racks to cool.

**To make the glaze,** in a small bowl, combine the confectioners' sugar, maple syrup, and milk. Drizzle over the cooled twists.

Alan Reid, Detroit, Michigan
*Michigan State Fair and Exposition, Detroit, Michigan*

# MICHIGAN STATE FAIR AND EXPOSITION
## Detroit, Michigan

M ichigan calls its state fair the oldest in the nation. Beginning in 1849, the Michigan State Fair was originally conceived to foster communication between rural agriculture and urban industry. Farmers saw the latest machinery, and city dwellers learned about produce and livestock. Today this practical approach has evolved into a rich blend of education, recreation, and entertainment. Attendance is well over 400,000, and 10,000 handcrafted, Michigan-made entries were displayed in 2003. Each year, some 100 animals are born at the fair's Blue Cross/Farm Bureau Birthing Center. This is a big attraction for children.

# Nutty Sweet Carrot Biscuits

*2 dozen biscuits*

2¾ cups flour
½ teaspoon ground cinnamon
4 teaspoons baking powder
½ teaspoon ground nutmeg
1¼ teaspoons salt
¾ cup chopped pecans or walnuts
2 cups mashed cooked carrots
1 teaspoon vanilla extract
¾ cup sugar
½ cup (1 stick) butter, melted

**Preheat** the oven to 450° F. In a large mixing bowl, combine the flour, cinnamon, baking powder, nutmeg, salt, and nuts. In another bowl, combine the carrots, vanilla, sugar, and butter. Add to the flour mixture and blend well. Turn out onto a lightly floured surface and knead slightly. Roll out to a ½-inch thickness. Cut with a 2½-inch biscuit cutter and place on a lightly greased baking sheet. Bake for 12 minutes, or until golden brown.

Emilie Dykes, Holtville, California
*Holtville Carrot Festival, Holtville, California*

For kitchen tips and more recipes, go to www.almanac.com/food.

# Barbara's Vidalia Muffins

*1 dozen regular-size muffins or 3 dozen mini-muffins*

Vegetable cooking spray
¾ cup milk
1 egg
⅓ cup vegetable oil
1 cup old-fashioned oats
1 cup self-rising flour
¼ cup sugar
½ cup chopped Vidalia onion
¾ cup shredded extra-sharp
   Cheddar cheese
⅓ cup broken pecans

**Preheat** the oven to 400° F. Grease the muffin cups with vegetable cooking spray. In a large bowl, beat the milk, egg, and oil. Stir in the oats, flour, and sugar just until moistened. Fold in the onion, cheese, and pecans. Divide the batter among the muffin cups. Bake for 18 to 20 minutes, or until a toothpick inserted in the center comes out clean. Best served warm.

Barbara T. Daniel, Reidsville, Georgia
*Vidalia Onion Cook-off, Vidalia Onion Festival, Vidalia, Georgia*

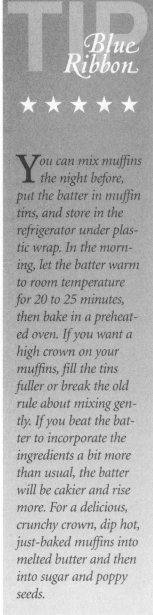

### Blue Ribbon

★ ★ ★ ★ ★

*You can mix muffins the night before, put the batter in muffin tins, and store in the refrigerator under plastic wrap. In the morning, let the batter warm to room temperature for 20 to 25 minutes, then bake in a preheated oven. If you want a high crown on your muffins, fill the tins fuller or break the old rule about mixing gently. If you beat the batter to incorporate the ingredients a bit more than usual, the batter will be cakier and rise more. For a delicious, crunchy crown, dip hot, just-baked muffins into melted butter and then into sugar and poppy seeds.*

# FLEMINGTON AGRICULTURAL FAIR

## Flemington, New Jersey

A t the Hunterdon County 4-H and Agricultural Fair, formerly the Flemington Agricultural Fair, you'll see the best of New Jersey's agricultural and 4-H exhibits. For five days and nights in late August, 40,000 people enjoy the country music, tractor pulls, championship horseshoe pitching, pig races, horse shows, midway rides, and other attractions at this old-fashioned fair.

# Feather Bed Potato Rolls

*16 to 20 rolls*

1 large potato, peeled and cut into 1-inch
 chunks
⅓ cup sugar
¼ cup (½ stick) butter, cut into pieces
1 teaspoon salt
1 package (1 tablespoon) dry yeast
1 egg
3¼ to 3¾ cups flour

**Boil** the potato until tender. Drain, reserving ¾ cup of the cooking water. Mash the potato and set aside.

**In a large bowl,** combine the hot potato cooking water, sugar, butter, and salt. Let stand until the butter is melted and the mixture is warm (105° to 115° F). Stir in the yeast and let stand for 5 to 10 minutes. Beat in the egg and potato by hand. Using a wooden spoon, stir in as much of the flour as you can. Turn the dough out onto a floured surface and knead for about 3 to 5 minutes, adding enough flour to make a moderately soft dough. Place in an oiled bowl, turning to coat all sides with oil. Cover and let rise in a warm place until doubled in bulk, about 1 to 1½ hours.

**Punch** the dough down. On a lightly floured surface, roll the dough out to a ½-inch thickness and cut with a 3-inch round cutter. Place the rounds ¼ inch apart on a lightly greased baking sheet. Cover and let rise until doubled in bulk, about 30 to 45 minutes.

**Preheat** the oven to 350° F. Bake for 18 to 20 minutes, or until golden brown. Remove to a wire rack to cool.

Kate Gallo, Princeton, New Jersey
*Flemington Agricultural Fair, Flemington, New Jersey*

**TIP**

*Blue Ribbon*

★ ★ ★ ★ ★

A*void beating eggs into any hot mixture, or they'll curdle.*

*Either cool the mixture first or add small amounts of the hot mixture to the eggs, beating well between additions. After the eggs are fairly well heated in this way, combine with remaining hot mixture and beat again.*

# Maple Nut Sweet Rolls

*16 twists*

## Dough

¾ cup milk
¼ cup (½ stick) butter
2¾ to 3 cups flour,
    divided
3 tablespoons sugar
½ teaspoon salt
1 package (1 tablespoon)
    dry yeast
¾ teaspoon maple extract
1 egg

## Filling

½ cup sugar
⅓ cup chopped walnuts
1 teaspoon ground cinnamon
¾ teaspoon maple extract
¼ cup (½ stick) butter, softened

## Glaze

1 cup confectioners' sugar
2 tablespoons butter, melted
1 tablespoon milk or water
½ teaspoon maple extract

**To make the dough,** heat the milk and butter in a small saucepan until warm. In a large bowl, combine the warm milk with 1 cup of the flour, sugar, salt, yeast, maple extract, and egg. Beat for 2 minutes with an electric mixer on medium speed. Stir in the remaining 1¾ to 2 cups flour by hand until the dough is elastic but not too dry. Knead the dough for a couple of minutes, or until soft. Cover and let rise for 45 to 60 minutes.

**To make the filling,** in a small bowl, combine the sugar, walnuts, cinnamon, and maple extract. Grease a 12-inch pizza pan. Divide the dough into 3 parts. Press one-third of the dough into the pan. Cover with one-third of the butter and one-third of the filling. Repeat the process with another two layers. Make slits from the center, cutting to form 16 rolls. Twist each roll. Cover and let rise for 30 to 45 minutes more.

**Preheat** the oven to 375° F. Bake for 18 to 22 minutes. Cool for 5 minutes and remove from the pan. Continue cooling on wire racks.

**To make the glaze,** in a small bowl, combine the confectioners' sugar, butter, milk or water, and maple extract. Mix until smooth. Drizzle over the twists.

Linda Brown, Easton, Maryland
*Delaware State Fair, Harrington, Delaware*

For more recipes and kitchen tips, go to www.almanac.com/food

# Squaw Bread

*2 loaves*

This recipe won first place in the "Whole-Wheat Bread" class and "Best in Category" for yeast breads.

**2 cups water**
**⅓ cup vegetable oil**
**½ cup plus 1 tablespoon honey**
**¼ cup raisins**
**2 packages (2 tablespoons) dry yeast**
**¼ cup warm water**
**2½ cups white flour, divided**
**3 cups whole-wheat flour, divided**
**1½ cups rye flour, divided**
**½ cup nonfat powdered milk**
**1½ teaspoons salt**

**In a blender,** combine the 2 cups water, oil, ½ cup honey, and raisins. Process to liquefy. In a small bowl, soften the yeast in the warm water and remaining 1 tablespoon honey. In a large bowl, combine 1 cup of the white flour, 2 cups of the whole-wheat flour, 1 cup of the rye flour, the water-raisin mixture, and the yeast mixture. Beat until smooth. Add the remaining 1½ cups white flour, 1 cup whole-wheat flour, and ½ cup rye flour, powdered milk, and salt. Mix until the dough is soft and pulls away from the sides of the bowl. Turn the dough out onto a floured surface and knead for 10 minutes. Place in an oiled bowl and let rise until doubled in bulk, about 45 minutes.

**Punch** the dough down and divide in half. Shape each piece into a rounded loaf. Place on a greased baking sheet and let rise until doubled in bulk, about 45 minutes. Preheat the oven to 350° F. Bake for 35 minutes, or until loaves sound hollow when tapped on top.

Dave Oxley, Seattle, Washington
*Western Washington Fair, Puyallup, Washington*

**TIP**

*Blue Ribbon*

★ ★ ★ ★ ★

**D**on't worry about overmixing bread dough if you are kneading by hand. But if you are using a food processor or mixer, you can overwork dough in about 20 minutes. Properly kneaded bread dough is elastic and looks satiny smooth. Overworked dough breaks down to become sticky and inelastic.

# French Bread with Spinach-Cheese Stuffing

*2 loaves*

*Dough*

1 package (1 tablespoon)
   dry yeast
2 teaspoons salt
2 cups warm water
2 tablespoons sugar
5 to 6 cups flour
Cornmeal

*Stuffing*

2 tablespoons butter
1 large onion, chopped

¾ cup cooked chopped spinach,
   squeezed dry
Pinch of freshly ground black
   pepper
1 teaspoon dill weed
1 teaspoon salt
6 ounces Swiss cheese, shredded

1 egg, beaten
Sesame seeds or poppy seeds
   (optional)

**To make the dough,** in a large bowl, combine the yeast, salt, water, sugar, and 5 cups of the flour. Knead the dough on a floured surface, adding flour until the dough is elastic but not too dry. Let rise in an oiled bowl until doubled in bulk, about 50 minutes. (The dough can be left to rise in the refrigerator overnight.) Knead again and divide into two oblong loaves. Sprinkle an oiled baking sheet with cornmeal. Place the loaves on the sheet. Let rise until doubled in bulk, about 50 minutes.

**Preheat** the oven to 350° F. To make the stuffing, melt the butter in a large skillet. Add the onion and sauté until tender. Add the spinach, pepper, dill weed, and salt. Add the cheese and cook until melted. Using a sharp knife, make a large slash in the top of each loaf and place the stuffing inside. Close the slash by pinching the dough. Brush the dough with the egg and sprinkle with sesame or poppy seeds (if using). Bake for 30 to 40 minutes, or until golden brown.

Kevin Coleman, Catarina, Texas
*Spinach Festival, Crystal City, Texas*

For more recipes and kitchen tips, go to www.almanac.com/food

# Chapter 8

Cakes & Pies

# LOUISIANA PECAN FESTIVAL

~

## Colfax, Louisiana

The Louisiana Pecan Festival began as part of the centennial celebration of Grant Parish in 1969 and has grown into an annual event. Always held the first weekend in November, it attracts 70,000 people. Each year, festivities begin with the blessing of the crops and move on to the Queen's Ball, where the Louisiana Pecan Festival Queen presides. Other events include a parade, a craft fair, log-cutting contests, a turkey shoot, a trail ride, a cooking competition, a street dance, and continuous live music. Colfax's railroad depot, over 100 years old, has been converted into a country store that stocks homegrown cornmeal, sugar cane, ribbon cane syrup, homemade preserves and candy, local handicrafts, and homegrown produce. Hoop cheese sliced to order is served with crackers and apple cider. Bulk pecans are available at the log Pecan House.

# Brown Mountain Pecan Cake

*8 to 10 servings*

## Cake

- 1 cup (2 sticks) butter
- 2 cups sugar
- 3 eggs
- 3 cups sifted flour
- 1 teaspoon baking soda
- ½ teaspoon salt
- 3 tablespoons unsweetened cocoa
- 1 cup buttermilk
- 1 teaspoon vanilla extract
- ½ cup warm water

## Frosting

- 1 package (8 ounces) cream cheese
- 1 box (1 pound) confectioners' sugar
- 2 tablespoons evaporated milk
- 6 teaspoons unsweetened cocoa
- 1 teaspoon almond extract

- 1½ cups pecans, coarsely chopped

**Preheat** the oven to 350° F.

**To make the cake,** in a large bowl, cream the butter and sugar until light and fluffy. Beat in the eggs one at a time. In another bowl, sift together the flour, baking soda, salt, and cocoa. Add the dry ingredients alternately with the buttermilk to the creamed mixture. Stir in the vanilla and water. Pour into three greased 9-inch cake pans. Bake for about 45 minutes, or until a tester inserted in the center comes out clean. Remove from the pans and cool on wire racks.

**To make the frosting,** in a large bowl, cream together the cream cheese and confectioners' sugar. Add the milk, cocoa, and almond extract and beat until smooth. Place one cake layer on a serving plate and top with frosting and one-third of the pecans. Repeat for the second layer. When the third layer is in place, frost the top and sides of the cake and decorate with the remaining pecans.

Emma Phillips, Colfax, Louisiana
*Louisiana Pecan Festival, Colfax, Louisiana*

# Carrot Cake with Creamy Pineapple Filling

*12 to 16 servings*

## Cake

2 cups sugar
1½ cups vegetable oil
4 eggs
2 cups flour
½ teaspoon baking soda
1½ teaspoons ground cinnamon
¼ teaspoon ground nutmeg
2 teaspoons baking powder
Pinch of salt
2 cups grated carrots
1 cup pecans or walnuts, chopped
1 can (8 ounces) unsweetened crushed pineapple, drained
2 tablespoons Grand Marnier

## Filling

1 can (20 ounces) unsweetened crushed pineapple with juice
¾ cup sugar
5 tablespoons flour
⅓ cup unsalted butter

## Frosting

½ cup (1 stick) unsalted butter, softened
1 package (8 ounces) cream cheese, softened
1 teaspoon vanilla extract
3 cups confectioners' sugar
2 teaspoons orange juice
2 teaspoons grated orange rind

Pecan halves or chopped walnuts for garnish (optional)

**Preheat** the oven to 350° F.

**To make the cake,** in the bowl of an electric mixer, beat the sugar and oil until creamy. Add the eggs one at a time, beating well after each addition until smooth and yellow, about 4 to 5 minutes. In a large bowl, sift together the flour, baking soda, cinnamon, nutmeg, baking powder, and salt. Add the flour mixture, a little at a time, to the sugar mixture, beating well after each addition. Add the carrots, nuts, pineapple, and Grand Marnier. Beat on low speed until well blended. Pour into three 8-inch cake pans that have been greased and dusted with flour. Bake for about 30 to 35 minutes, or until a toothpick inserted in the center comes out clean. Cool in the pans for 10 minutes before turning out onto wire racks.

**To make the filling,** in a medium saucepan, combine the pineapple, sugar, flour, and butter. Cook over medium heat, stirring constantly, until thickened. Remove from the heat and cool completely.

For kitchen tips and more recipes, go to www.almanac.com/food.

**To make the frosting,** in a medium bowl, cream the butter and cream cheese until fluffy. Add the vanilla, confectioners' sugar, orange juice, and orange rind. Mix until smooth.

**To assemble the cake,** place one cake layer on a serving plate and spread half the pineapple filling on top. Add another layer and spread the remaining filling on top. Add the third layer and spread the frosting over the top and sides of the cake. Decorate with pecan halves or chopped walnuts if desired. Refrigerate until ready to serve.

Dorothy Lacefield, Carrollton, Texas
*"Best of Show" Cake Contest, State Fair of Texas, Dallas, Texas*

# "Best of Show" Chocolate Cake

*1 bundt cake*

| | |
|---|---|
| 1¾ cups flour | 2 eggs |
| 2 cups sugar | 1 cup milk |
| ¾ cup imported cocoa | ½ cup vegetable oil |
| 1½ teaspoons baking soda | 2 teaspoons vanilla extract |
| 1½ teaspoons baking powder | 1 cup boiling water |
| 1 teaspoon salt | |

**Preheat** the oven to 350° F. In a large bowl, combine the flour, sugar, cocoa, baking soda, baking powder, and salt. Mix well. Add the eggs, milk, oil, and vanilla. With an electric mixer, beat at medium speed for 2 minutes. Stir in the boiling water by hand. The batter will be thin. Pour into a greased bundt pan and bake for 40 minutes, or until a tester inserted in the cake comes out clean. Cool for 10 minutes in the pan on a wire rack, then remove from the pan and continue cooling on the rack. The cake will be very moist.

Diane Morrison, Flemington, New Jersey
*Flemington Agricultural Fair, Flemington, New Jersey*

# Blueberry Jelly Roll

*10 servings*

Cathy Poluzzi has won three blue ribbons with this recipe. She fills the cake with her own homemade blueberry jam. The "key to success with this recipe," says Cathy, "is to beat the eggs like crazy. I use my KitchenAid mixer on a setting of 6 or 8 and beat for nearly 5 minutes—this gives the light texture."

> 5 medium eggs, at room temperature
> 1 cup sugar
> 1 tablespoon fresh lemon juice
> 1 teaspoon vanilla extract
> 1 cup cake flour
> Confectioners' sugar
> ½ cup blueberry jam

**Preheat** the oven to 350° F. In a medium bowl, beat the eggs, sugar, and lemon juice until pale and fluffy, about 5 minutes. Add the vanilla and blend in the flour. Do not overbeat.

**Grease** a 10x15x1-inch jelly-roll pan with butter, then line with wax paper and butter the wax paper. Pour in the batter and gently tap the pan to remove any bubbles. Bake for 18 to 20 minutes, or until golden and the sides pull away from the pan.

**Sprinkle** paper towels with confectioners' sugar and turn the cake out onto them. Let cool. Spread the cake with the jam, roll up, and sprinkle again with confectioners' sugar. Slice each end on an angle, just enough to even the sides of the roll and give it a nice look.

Catherine Poluzzi, Poughkeepsie, New York
*Dutchess County Fair, Rhinebeck, New York*

For kitchen tips and more recipes, go to www.almanac.com/food.

# Chocolate-Amaretto Cheesecake

*12 servings*

1½ cups finely crushed chocolate wafers
⅓ cup butter, melted
3 packages (8 ounces each) cream cheese, softened
1½ cups sugar
4 squares (4 ounces) semisweet chocolate, melted and cooled
2 tablespoons flour
1 teaspoon vanilla extract
4 eggs
¼ cup milk
¼ cup amaretto
1 square (1 ounce) semisweet chocolate, shaved in curls, for garnish

**Preheat** the oven to 350° F. In a medium bowl, combine the crushed wafers and butter. Press evenly over the bottom and up the sides of a 9-inch springform pan. Place the pan in a shallow baking dish.

**In a large mixer bowl,** beat the cream cheese, sugar, melted chocolate, flour, and vanilla until well mixed. Add the eggs all at once, then beat with an electric mixer on low speed just until mixed. Do not overbeat. Stir in the milk and amaretto. Pour into the crust and bake for about 45 minutes, or until the center appears nearly set when gently shaken. Cool on a wire rack for 5 to 10 minutes. Loosen the sides of the cheesecake from the pan. Cool for 30 minutes more before removing the sides of the pan. Cover and chill overnight. Before serving, garnish with chocolate curls.

Sandra Perry, Pittsfield, Maine
*Central Maine Egg Festival, Pittsfield, Maine*

# Missouri Walnut Pie

*8 servings*

Sue Jones, who has been an exhibitor at the Ozark Empire Fair for many years, says, "Two times I've entered this recipe in the Hammons Black Walnut Cooking Contest at the fair, and each time I've won the blue ribbon!"

- 3 eggs, slightly beaten
- 1 cup sugar
- 2 tablespoons flour
- 1 cup dark corn syrup
- 2 tablespoons butter, melted
- 1 teaspoon vanilla extract
- Pastry for single-crust 9-inch pie
- 1½ cups black walnuts or regular walnuts, broken

**Preheat** the oven to 400° F. In a medium bowl, combine the eggs, sugar, flour, corn syrup, butter, and vanilla. Blend well. Line a 9-inch pie plate with the pastry. Pour the filling into the crust. Arrange the walnuts on top. Bake in the lower third of the oven for 15 minutes. Reduce the oven temperature to 350° F and bake for 35 to 40 minutes more, or until the center appears set. Cool completely before serving.

Sue Jones, Springfield, Missouri
*Hammons Black Walnut Cooking Contest,*
*Ozark Empire Fair,*
*Springfield, Missouri*

# Hammons Black Walnut Cooking Contest

## Ozark Empire Fair
### Springfield, Missouri

According to Hammons Products, the largest processor of eastern black walnuts in the world, the taste and flavor of their nuts is unlike that of English or California walnuts. Eastern black walnuts have an aroma (the others have little) and a rich, nutty taste that comes alive in cookies, brownies, breads, cakes, and pies. Cooks throughout the Midwest and South have enjoyed a long tradition of baking with eastern black walnuts. Hammons Products, which began in 1946, is a family-owned and -managed company. In addition to shell processing, the company uses discarded nutmeats to produce animal feed, has a land management division to help landowners develop black walnut trees into a cash crop, and runs a mail-order and retail shop, the Black Walnut Emporium, which offers a variety of nutmeats and specialty gift items.

# Cherry Mocha Mousse Pie

*12 servings*

3 cups chocolate wafer crumbs
⅓ cup margarine, melted
1 can (21 ounces) cherry pie filling, divided
¼ cup sugar
1 envelope unflavored gelatin
1 cup cold water
3 squares (3 ounces) white baking bar with cocoa butter,
    chopped
3 egg yolks
1½ cups heavy cream
2 tablespoons coffee liqueur
Whipped cream and chocolate shavings for garnish (optional)

**Preheat** the oven to 350° F. Lightly butter the bottom and sides of a 10-inch pie plate. In a large bowl, combine the wafer crumbs and margarine. Press the mixture firmly against the bottom and sides of the pie plate. Bake for 8 minutes. When the crust is cool, spread ½ cup of the cherry pie filling evenly over the bottom and chill. Refrigerate the remaining filling until serving time.

**In a medium saucepan,** combine the sugar and gelatin; mix well. Add the water and white baking bar. Bring to a boil over medium heat, stirring constantly, and cook until the gelatin is completely dissolved. In a small bowl, beat the egg yolks. Add 1 cup of the hot gelatin mixture to the yolks and quickly stir until combined. Return to the saucepan and cook over medium heat, stirring constantly, until the mixture bubbles. Transfer the gelatin mixture to a large bowl. Chill in the refrigerator, stirring occasionally, for 45 minutes or until it is the consistency of unbeaten egg whites. Do not let it get too firm.

**Meanwhile,** in the chilled bowl of an electric mixer, beat the cream until stiff peaks form. Add the liqueur. Gently fold into the chilled gelatin mixture. Pour into the crust. Cover and refrigerate overnight. Just before serving, spoon the remaining cherry filling evenly over the pie and garnish with whipped cream and chocolate shavings if desired.

Richard Rizzio, Traverse City, Michigan
*National Cherry Festival, Traverse City, Michigan*

# Pumpkin Pie with Cookie Nut Crust

*8 servings*

1¼ cups flour
¼ teaspoon baking soda
½ cup (1 stick) margarine, softened
½ cup loosely packed brown sugar
½ cup finely chopped walnuts
½ teaspoon vanilla extract
1½ tablespoons cornstarch
½ teaspoon ground cinnamon
½ teaspoon ground ginger
¼ teaspoon ground nutmeg
1 scant cup granulated sugar
1 can (15 ounces) pumpkin
1½ cups light cream
2 eggs
2 tablespoons molasses

**Preheat** the oven to 350° F. In a large bowl, combine the flour and baking soda. Add the margarine, brown sugar, walnuts, and vanilla. Blend well. Press the mixture, a small amount at a time, into a 9-inch pie plate, building up the sides and fluting the edge. Cover the fluting with a strip of aluminum foil to prevent overbrowning.

**In another bowl,** thoroughly combine the cornstarch, cinnamon, ginger, nutmeg, and granulated sugar. Add the pumpkin, cream, eggs, and molasses. Pour into the crust and bake for 1 to 1½ hours, or until the center is set.

Mary Schwartz, Lunenburg, Massachusetts
*Bolton Fair, Bolton, Massachusetts*

# Machias Wild Blueberry Festival

## Machias, Maine

Folks in Machias will tell you that the blueberries grown in the barrens of Washington County, Maine, are smaller and more flavorful than the high-bush cultivated blueberries of New Jersey and Michigan. Cooks say that Maine wild blueberries have a distinctive taste and firmer skin that allows them to retain their shape and juice better in the heat of the oven. If you'd like a taste test, try the muffins, pies, pancakes, ice cream, buckles, slumps, crisps, and cakes at the Machias Wild Blueberry Festival, held during the third weekend in August. The Centre Street Congregational Church started the festival 29 years ago to "show thanks to God for the continuing harvest of luscious and nutritious blueberries that have improved the economic and physical health of all of us for more than 100 years." Now, 15,000 people attend the annual event, enjoying Friday night's Downeast fish fry, Saturday morning's pancake breakfast, and the blueberry run, craft fair, book sale, raffle of a one-of-a-kind blueberry quilt, parade, band concert, cook-off, and pie-eating contest.

# Blueberry-Lemon Wisp

*10 to 12 servings*

### Crust

2 cups crushed gingersnaps
½ cup finely chopped pecans
⅓ cup butter, melted
1 teaspoon ground cinnamon
1 tablespoon brown sugar

### Filling

2 envelopes unflavored gelatin
½ cup orange juice
1 pint Maine wild blueberries
2 packages (8 ounces each) light
  cream cheese
1 container (8 ounces) low-fat
  blueberry yogurt

1 container (8 ounces) low-fat
  lemon yogurt
½ cup sugar
1 teaspoon vanilla extract
1 teaspoon lemon juice

### Topping

1 cup whipping cream
4 to 5 tablespoons confectioners'
  sugar
2 teaspoons lemon juice

Grated lemon rind for garnish

**Preheat** the oven to 350° F.

**To make the crust,** in a medium bowl, combine the gingersnaps, pecans, butter, cinnamon, and brown sugar, mixing well with a fork. Pat evenly into a 10-inch spring-form pan. Bake for 10 minutes, or until lightly browned.

**To make the filling,** in a small saucepan over low heat, dissolve the gelatin in the orange juice, stirring until completely dissolved. Rinse the blueberries, drain, and set aside. Reserve ½ cup for garnish. In a medium bowl, blend the cream cheese, blueberry and lemon yogurts, sugar, vanilla, and lemon juice. With the electric mixer running at low speed, slowly add the orange juice–gelatin mixture. Mix at medium speed for about 2 minutes. Gently fold in the blueberries by hand. Pour into the prepared crust and chill for several hours until set.

**To make the topping,** in a small bowl, whip the cream until stiff and slowly blend in the confectioners' sugar and lemon juice. To serve, gently run a knife around the rim of the springform pan. Remove the outside form and transfer the wisp to a serving plate. Using a pastry bag, pipe the whipped cream around the base and top of the cake. Garnish with the reserved blueberries and grated lemon rind.

Kathleen Fritz, Machias, Maine
*Machias Wild Blueberry Festival, Machias, Maine*

# Mom's Chess Pie

*8 servings*

This recipe is from Andrea White's mother, Fredia Hankins, who lives in Muncie. Andrea has entered Chess Pie in many competitions and always places with her mom's recipe.

1½ cups sugar
½ cup (1 stick) butter
2 eggs
½ cup milk
2 tablespoons flour
1 tablespoon cornmeal
Pinch of salt
1 teaspoon vanilla extract
1 teaspoon white vinegar
1 teaspoon whiskey
Pastry for single-crust 9-inch pie

**Preheat** the oven to 400° F. In a large bowl, cream the sugar and butter and blend in the eggs. Add the milk, flour, cornmeal, salt, vanilla, vinegar, and whiskey, blending well after each addition. Line a 9-inch pie plate with the pastry. Pour the filling into the crust. Bake for 10 minutes. Reduce the temperature to 350° F and bake for about 30 minutes more, or until a knife inserted in the center comes out clean.

Andrea White, Indianapolis, Indiana
*Indiana State Fair, Indianapolis, Indiana*

# INDIANA STATE FAIR

## Indianapolis, Indiana

The Indiana State Fair began in 1852. During the Civil War, the fairgrounds became Camp Morton, a prisoner-of-war camp for Confederate soldiers. Through the years, the fair has attracted John Philip Sousa, Woodrow Wilson, Franklin Delano Roosevelt, John F. Kennedy, Elvis Presley, Frank Sinatra, the Beatles, and millions of fair-goers. The Indiana 4-H program, highlighting the talent of Hoosier youths, is a major attraction. Perennial favorites, as described by fair organizers, include the world's largest boar, rooster crowing contests, an 18-hole agricultural miniature golf course, a pioneer village, championship harness racing, and the largest draft-horse show in the Western Hemisphere.

# Red and Gold Delight

*6 to 8 servings*

*Filling*

> **2 cups sliced fresh peaches**
> **2 cups fresh raspberries**
> **1 cup sugar**
> **1 tablespoon lemon juice**
> **2 to 4 tablespoons quick-cooking tapioca**
> **(depending on juiciness of fruit)**

*Crust*

> **2 cups flour**
> **1 teaspoon salt**
> **1 cup butter-flavored shortening**
> **4 to 6 tablespoons ice water**

**In a large bowl,** gently combine the peaches, raspberries, and sugar. Sprinkle the lemon juice over the fruit and stir in the tapioca. Let stand for 15 minutes.

**Meanwhile,** make the crust. Preheat the oven to 400° F. Place the flour and salt in a large bowl. Cut in the shortening until the mixture resembles coarse cornmeal. Gradually add the ice water, 1 tablespoon at a time. Gently toss the flour with a fork to dampen. Gather the dough into a ball and chill for 10 minutes. Divide the dough in half. Roll out one half on a floured surface and line a 9-inch pie plate with it. Pour the filling into the crust. Roll out the remaining dough and cut into ¾-inch-wide strips. Twist each strip and lay it on top of the filling. Bake for 1 hour, or until golden brown.

Brenda Brekke, Federal Way, Washington
*Western Washington Fair, Puyallup, Washington*

For kitchen tips and more recipes, go to www.almanac.com/food.

Chapter 9

# Cookies & Candies

# Vermont Dairy Festival

~

## Enosburg Falls, Vermont

The 48-year-old Vermont Dairy Festival is held for four days over the first full weekend in June. Sponsored by the Lions Club, it draws 50,000 people and is one of the largest annual events in the state. Most activities take place on the village green of Enosburg Falls. On Saturday, there is a big parade with bands from Vermont and Canada, a road race, a chicken barbecue, tractor and horse pulls, milking contests, a craft show, and country-and-western entertainment. The dairy-cooking contest is open to Vermont residents of all ages. Each entrant must prepare a dish using a significant amount of a Vermont dairy product. Judges award up to 75 points for accuracy of recipe, appearance, quality and taste, texture, uniformity of shape and size, and use of Vermont dairy products.

# Cheesy Dapper Apple Squares

*16 squares*

1½ cups flour
1½ cups graham cracker crumbs
1 cup firmly packed brown sugar
½ teaspoon baking soda
¾ cup (1½ sticks) butter, softened
6 ounces Cheddar cheese, thinly sliced
2½ cups baking apples, cored, peeled, and sliced
¾ cup granulated sugar
½ cup chopped walnuts

**Preheat** the oven to 350° F. In a large bowl, mix together the flour, graham cracker crumbs, brown sugar, baking soda, and butter. Set aside 1½ cups of the crumb mixture and pat the rest into an ungreased 9x13-inch baking dish. Place the cheese slices on top of the crumb mixture.

**In a medium bowl,** combine the apples and granulated sugar. Layer over the cheese. Add the nuts to the reserved crumb mixture and sprinkle over the apples. Bake for 35 to 40 minutes, or until golden brown. Cool completely, then cut into 2-inch squares. This can be served as a side dish with bean soup or as a dessert.

Richard Pudvah, Enosburg Falls, Vermont
*Vermont Dairy Festival, Enosburg Falls, Vermont*

# Gingersnap Cookies

*4 dozen cookies*

¾ cup (1½ sticks) butter
1 cup sugar
¼ cup molasses
1 egg, well beaten
2 cups flour
2 teaspoons baking soda
1 teaspoon ground cinnamon
1 teaspoon ground ginger
1 teaspoon ground cloves
Sugar for dipping

**Preheat** the oven to 350° F. In a large bowl, thoroughly cream the butter and sugar. Add the molasses and egg and blend well. Add the flour, baking soda, cinnamon, ginger, and cloves, and blend until smooth. Roll into small balls and dip in sugar. Flatten the balls and place 2 inches apart on ungreased cookie sheets. Bake for 7 to 10 minutes. Remove from the sheets and cool on wire racks.

Jean Thomas, Buchanan, Virginia
*Salem Fair, Salem, Virginia*

## TIP
### *Blue Ribbon*
★ ★ ★ ★ ★

For easy cleanup and even browning, try lining cookie sheets with parchment or aluminum foil (shiny side up). Invest in an oven thermometer and take your oven's temperature after it has preheated for 20 minutes. Adjust accordingly to achieve the recommended temperature.

It is easy to overmix cookie dough with an electric mixer. For best results, mix only until the ingredients are combined. For old-fashioned chewy cookies, mix the dough by hand.

For kitchen tips and more recipes, go to www.almanac.com/food.

# Chocolate Caramel Cookies

*4 dozen cookies*

Candy coating chips can be found in party supply stores.

**7 tablespoons butter**
**¼ cup sugar**
**½ teaspoon vanilla extract**
**¼ cup old-fashioned oats**
**¾ cup flour**
**2 tablespoons cocoa**
**¼ cup finely chopped pecans**
**25 caramel candies**
**1½ tablespoons milk**
**2 cups milk chocolate candy coating chips**
**2 tablespoons white chocolate candy coating chips**

**Preheat** the oven to 375° F. In a large bowl, cream the butter and sugar. Add the vanilla. In a separate bowl, combine the oats, flour, and cocoa. Add to the butter mixture. Stir in the pecans. Turn the dough out onto a floured surface and pat to a ⅛-inch thickness. Cut with a 1-inch round cookie cutter. (If you don't have one this size, use a well-floured bottle cap.) Place on ungreased cookie sheets. Bake for 10 to 12 minutes. Remove from the sheets and cool on wire racks.

**While the cookies are cooling,** in a medium saucepan, melt the caramels with the milk. Stir until smooth. Place about ½ teaspoon caramel on top of one cookie and top with another cookie. (If the caramel runs off the cookie, wait a couple of minutes for it to thicken.) Chill for about 15 minutes to set the caramel.

**Melt** the milk chocolate chips in the microwave or the top of a double boiler until smooth. If you're using the microwave, place the chocolate in a shallow bowl, heat for 1 minute, stir, heat for 30 seconds more, and stir. The chocolate will be more melted than it looks; don't burn it! Remove the cookies from the refrigerator and dip each cookie in melted chocolate. Place on wax paper to cool.

**Melt** the white chocolate chips in the microwave for 45 seconds or the top of a double boiler. Drizzle each cookie with a light band of white chocolate.

Joan Randall, Kelley, Iowa
*Iowa State Fair, Des Moines, Iowa*

# Citrus Cookies

*3 dozen cookies*

### Cookies

**1⅔ cups flour**
**⅓ cup confectioners' sugar**
**1 cup (2 sticks) butter**
**1 teaspoon lemon extract**
**1 teaspoon grated lemon rind**

### Frosting

**2 cups confectioners' sugar**
**1 tablespoon butter**
**1 tablespoon lemon juice**
**Yellow food coloring**

**Preheat** the oven to 350° F.

**To make the cookies,** in a medium bowl, combine the flour, confectioners' sugar, butter, lemon extract, and lemon rind. Mix well. Roll the dough into 1-inch balls. Place the cookies 1 inch apart on cookie sheets lined with parchment paper. With your thumb, make an imprint in the center of each cookie. Bake for 8 to 10 minutes, or until lightly browned. Remove from the sheets and cool on wire racks.

**To make the frosting,** in a medium bowl, beat together the confectioners' sugar, butter, lemon juice, and enough food coloring to make the frosting pale yellow. When the cookies are cool, place a dollop of frosting in the center of each one.

Beth Sternitsky, Apache Junction, Arizona
*Arizona State Fair, Phoenix, Arizona*

## ARIZONA STATE FAIR

### Phoenix, Arizona

The Arizona State Fair originated in 1884 as a territorial fair and has been presented nearly every year since. Today 1 million fair-goers enjoy activities such as 4-H clogging, baton twirling, rodeos, livestock shows, pie-eating contests, and continuous live entertainment.

# Luella Larson's Spritz Cookies

*8 dozen cookies*

1 cup sugar
2 cups (4 sticks) butter
1 egg
¼ teaspoon salt
4 to 4½ cups flour
1 teaspoon almond extract

**Preheat** the oven to 350° F. In a large bowl, cream the sugar and butter together until the mixture is light and fluffy. With an electric mixer set at moderate speed, blend in the egg and salt. Mix in the flour a little at a time until the batter is stiff but not dry. Beat in the almond extract. (Do not refrigerate the dough; it is best when soft.) Pack the dough into a cookie press with a ring. Press the cookies out onto two ungreased cookie sheets. Bake for 10 to 15 minutes, or until the cookies are golden and lightly browned on the edges. Remove from the sheets and cool on wire racks.

Luella Larson, Crooks, South Dakota
*Sioux Empire Fair, Sioux Falls, South Dakota*

# Easy No-Bake Praline Cookies

*4 dozen cookies*

Vegetable cooking spray
1 packet plus 1 square graham crackers
1 cup (2 sticks) butter (do not use margarine)
½ cup sugar
1½ cups chopped pecans

**Spray** vegetable cooking spray onto a cookie sheet with sides. Line the cookie sheet with the graham crackers so that the crackers are touching one another. Melt the butter in a saucepan, add the sugar, and boil for exactly 2 minutes. Pour over the graham crackers and sprinkle with the pecans. When the bubbling stops, cut into pieces and put on a wire rack to cool.

Nancy Sasso, Hurst, Texas
*"Best of Show," Cookie Contest, State Fair of Texas, Dallas, Texas*

# Black Walnut Toffee Bars

*20 bars*

2 cups flour
½ cup confectioners' sugar
1 cup (2 sticks) butter
1 can (14 ounces) sweetened condensed milk
1 egg
1 teaspoon vanilla extract
½ teaspoon salt
1 package (6 ounces) toffee chips
1 cup black walnuts or regular walnuts, chopped

**Preheat** the oven to 350° F. In a medium bowl, combine the flour and confectioners' sugar. Cut in the butter. Press into a 9x13-inch baking dish. Bake for 15 minutes.

**While the crust is baking,** in a medium bowl, beat the milk, egg, vanilla, and salt. Stir in the toffee chips and walnuts. Spread over the cooked crust and bake for 18 to 25 minutes. Cool completely, then cut into 2-inch bars.

Leisa J. Lower, Springfield, Missouri
*Ozark Empire Fair, Springfield, Missouri*

## Ozark Empire Fair

### Springfield, Missouri

For 69 years, the Ozark Empire Fair has celebrated the local agriculture of southwestern Missouri and the creativity of the region's craftspeople. The crafts and foods divisions are very popular, receiving thousands of entries each year.

# NATIONAL DATE FESTIVAL

## Indio, California

**P**romoters of the National Date Festival call it "America's most exotic fair," and they may well be right. Where else can you see camel and ostrich races and a nightly musical revue featuring singers, dancers, and exotic animals depicting a marketplace in old Baghdad? The Riverside County Fair and National Date Festival officially began at its present site in 1947 and has become southern California's biggest annual winter event, attracting nearly 275,000 visitors each February. The date industry is on hand with samples and treats to eat. Date classes in the competition handbook read like something out of the Arabian Nights: Abbada, Amir Hajj, Barhi, Dayri, Deglet Noor, Halawi, Khadrawi, Maktoom, Medjool, Tabarazal, Tazizoot, Zahidi, and others.

The Coachella Valley, located in the desert of southern California, is the heart of America's date industry. Many varieties grow there. Semidry dates such as Deglet Noor and Zahidi are good for snacking, cooking, and baking. Soft dates such as Medjool, Khadrawi, and Halawi are great for sauces and snacks. California dates have the right balance of sugar and moisture to keep year-round. If placed in an airtight container and stored in the refrigerator (40° F), dates will stay moist and delicious for up to a year. Dates also can be frozen almost indefinitely with no loss of quality. If moisture is lost during storage, simply soak or steam dates in warm water, fruit juice, or liquor.

# Stuffed Dates

*2 dozen dates*

In 1996, Dorothy Dillon entered 100 dishes at the fair, hoping to win enough prize money to buy her mother a freezer and clothes dryer. Dorothy happily reported that she earned more than $500, which she used to purchase the appliances for her mom, Jean Branson.

24 pitted dates
2 cups sugar
½ cup hot water
½ cup light corn syrup
2 egg whites
1 cup chopped walnuts or pecans
1 teaspoon vanilla extract

**Slice** the dates down the center, being careful not to cut through. Place the sugar, water, and corn syrup in a medium saucepan and cook over medium heat, stirring constantly, until you can spin thread. Whip the egg whites until stiff peaks form. Remove half the cooked syrup and add to the egg whites, blending well. Cook the remaining syrup to the hard-ball stage (255° F). Add the nuts and vanilla; mix well. Add this mixture to the egg white mixture and beat until stiff but not dry. Place 1 teaspoon of filling in the center of each date. Wrap with plastic and store in an airtight container.

Dorothy Dillon, Indio, California
*National Date Festival, Indio, California*

# Peanut Brittle

*10x12-inch sheet*

1 cup sugar
½ cup light corn syrup
¼ cup water
2 cups raw peanuts
1 tablespoon baking soda

**Line** a 10x12-inch cookie sheet with heavy-duty aluminum foil. In a heavy pot, mix together the sugar, corn syrup, and water. Bring to a boil over medium heat. Add the peanuts. Cook, stirring often, until the peanuts smell parched, about 15 minutes. Add the baking soda and stir quickly. The mixture will foam, then turn a golden color. Quickly pour on the foil-lined cookie sheet. When cool, break into pieces.

Linda Collier, Perry, Georgia
*Georgia National Fair, Perry, Georgia*

For kitchen tips and more recipes, go to www.almanac.com/food.

# Ohio Buckeyes

*5 dozen buckeyes*

Ruth Cahill has made thousands of buckeyes over the years. For winning a blue ribbon at the Ohio State Fair, she was one of a handful of cooks invited to New York for the Citymeals-on-Wheels benefit, where bakers made 500 of her buckeyes as part of the fund-raising dinner.

> 1 cup (2 sticks) butter, at room temperature
> 1 jar (16 ounces) peanut butter (smooth or chunky)
> 1½ boxes (1½ pounds) confectioners' sugar (approximately)
> 1 package (12 ounces) semisweet chocolate chips
> 2 squares (2 ounces) semisweet chocolate
> ¼ bar paraffin*

**In a medium bowl,** blend the butter, peanut butter, and confectioners' sugar until smooth. (You may need to adjust the amount of sugar depending on the brand of peanut butter you use. Jif extra crunchy works perfectly with the measurements given.) Roll into 1-inch balls. Chill thoroughly.

**Melt the chocolate chips,** semisweet chocolate, and paraffin in the top of a double boiler or a pan set over hot water (the water should not boil). Use a small-bottomed pan, which will keep the chocolate deep for dipping. Using a toothpick or thin skewer, dip the peanut butter balls in the melted chocolate. Leave an "eye" undipped at the top of the ball so that it resembles a buckeye. If the coating is thick, you might have to prepare a second batch of chocolate. Chill to set the chocolate.

Ruth Cahill, Columbus, Ohio
*Ohio State Fair, Columbus, Ohio*

*\*Buckeyes are a traditional Ohio candy, and all the old recipes call for paraffin, which helps the chocolate keep its shape. Here is another method of stabilizing the chocolate with part solid chips:*

Prepare the peanut butter filling as above. Put 4 squares (4 ounces) semisweet chocolate and all but ¼ cup of a 12-ounce package of semisweet chocolate chips in the top of a double boiler. Heat, stirring well, until thoroughly melted. Remove from the heat and quickly stir in the reserved chips. Stir continuously until the chocolate is cooled to 90° F for dark chocolate, 88° F for milk and white chocolate. If you don't have a thermometer, try the "mustache test": Drip a little chocolate on your upper lip; if it feels cool, it is the right temperature.

Recipe adaptation courtesy of Nur Kilic,
*owner of Serenade Chocolatier in Brookline, Massachusetts*

# Quick Cranberry Nut Fudge

*3 dozen pieces*

**2 packages (12 ounces each) semisweet chocolate chips**
**1 package (6 ounces) sweetened cranberries**
**1 can (14 ounces) sweetened condensed milk**
**1 teaspoon vanilla extract**
**½ cup chopped walnuts or pecans**

**Melt** the chocolate chips until smooth in the microwave or in a saucepan. Stir in the cranberries, milk, vanilla, and nuts. Pour into a buttered 10x7-inch pan. After the fudge has solidified, cut into 1-inch pieces.

Delrolyn St. Louis, Freetown, Massachusetts
*Cranberry Harvest Festival, Carver, Massachusetts*

# Chapter 10

## Pickles & Preserves

# COMMON GROUND COUNTRY FAIR

## Windsor, Maine

Twenty years ago, the Maine Organic Farmers and Gardeners Association organized a fair to provide a common ground for people to share their knowledge. Today the Common Ground Country Fair, always held in late September, has an annual attendance of 50,000 people and more than 1,000 working volunteers. Visitors learn about organic farming and new composting techniques, hear from experts in the field, and are entertained with live music, fiddling contests, pig-calling contests, sheepdog demonstrations, children's crafts, and more. Pickled fiddleheads, smoked dulse, and Penobscot porridge are just a few of the local delicacies that can be purchased. Booths display wool, mohair, angora, dried flowers, herbs, spices, mustards, grains, baking mixes, and heirloom and organic seeds.

Visitors are encouraged to car-pool and bike to the fair to save on parking and fuel, and the fair strives to achieve zero garbage generation. Food vendors, for example, use recyclable or compostable plates and packaging whenever possible, and disposable diapers are discouraged. At the 1994 fair, more than 24,300 pounds of food scraps, paper products, and wood were recovered and composted with manure and other organic matter into a nutrient-rich soil amendment.

# Janet's Zucchini Relish

*3 ½ pints*

Amy LeBlanc credits this recipe to her best friend, Janet Bedard, whose family has handed it down through a couple of generations. This relish repeatedly wins blue ribbons whenever it is entered at the fair. Amy is an organic gardener and inspector who has been selling her preserves and vinegars for ten years. In her recipe for Golden Peach Salsa (see page 134), adapted from the *Ball Blue Book* (31st ed.), Amy substituted 2 cups peaches for 2 cups tomatoes and used some 'Golden Boy', 'Hillbilly', and 'Yellow Perfection' tomatoes instead of red fruits. The result was a "glorious golden salsa."

    10 cups grated zucchini
    5 medium onions, chopped
    ½ cup chopped red bell pepper
    1 cup chopped green bell pepper
    2 large tomatoes, chopped
    3 large stalks celery, diced
    ½ cup salt
    2½ cups white vinegar
    4 cups sugar
    2 teaspoons freshly ground black pepper
    1¼ teaspoons powdered mustard
    1 teaspoon turmeric
    1 teaspoon ground allspice
    2½ teaspoons celery seed
    1 tablespoon cornstarch dissolved in ¼ cup cool water

**In a large glass or stainless steel bowl,** combine the zucchini, onion, red and green peppers, tomatoes, and celery. Add the salt and stir well. Place a plate directly on the vegetables and press down (a stack of smaller bowls works well). Let stand overnight.

**In the morning,** drain the vegetables and rinse well two or three times, until most of the salty taste is gone. Transfer to a large stainless steel pot and add the vinegar, sugar, black pepper, mustard, turmeric, allspice, celery seed, and cornstarch-water mixture. Stir well. Simmer for 45 minutes, or until the sauce is clear. Fill ½-pint or 1-pint jars with the relish, cover, and process in a boiling-water bath for 10 minutes for ½-pint jars or 15 minutes for 1-pint jars.

Amy LeBlanc, East Wilton, Maine
*Common Ground Country Fair, Windsor, Maine*

# Golden Peach Salsa

*3 pints*

**2 cups peeled, cored, and chopped tomatoes**
**2 cups peeled, pitted, and chopped peaches**
**2 cups seeded and chopped green bell pepper**
**1 cup seeded and chopped chili or jalapeño pepper**
**¾ cup chopped onion**
**1½ teaspoons salt**
**2 cloves garlic, minced**
**1½ cups apple cider vinegar**

**Combine** the tomatoes, peaches, bell pepper, hot pepper, onion, salt, garlic, and vinegar in a large saucepot. Bring to a boil. Reduce the heat and simmer for about 20 minutes. Pour into hot, sterilized jars, leaving a ¼-inch headspace. Adjust the caps and process in a boiling-water bath for 30 minutes.

Amy LeBlanc, East Wilton, Maine
*Common Ground Country Fair, Windsor, Maine*

# Shaker Dilly Beans

*8 pints*

    **4 pounds fresh green beans, washed and trimmed**
    **8 teaspoons dill seed, divided**
    **4 teaspoons mustard seed, divided**
    **8 cloves garlic (or more, to taste), divided**
    **5 cups white vinegar**
    **5 cups water**
    **½ cup salt**

**Cut** the beans so that they fit in pint jars. Prepare the jars by rinsing them with hot water. Fill with the beans, stacking them lengthwise. To each jar, add 1 teaspoon dill seed, ½ teaspoon mustard seed, and 1 clove garlic cut in half. In a large pot, combine the vinegar, water, and salt. Heat to boiling. Pour the boiling solution over the beans, filling to within ½ inch of the top of the jar. Process in a boiling-water bath, tighten the lids if necessary, and cool. Store in a cool place for at least two weeks for the beans to develop their full flavor.

Sister Frances Carr, Shaker Society, New Gloucester, Maine
*Common Ground Country Fair, Windsor, Maine*

# Grandmother Lida Quinn's Pickled Beets

*6 pints*

Becky Quinn reports, "These pickled beets have a good combination of sweet and sour tastes and because of this have won first place at five different Ozark Empire Fairs." Becky, who learned to can at her grandmother's side starting when she was 6 years old, often makes this recipe three times during the summer. "I could make these in my sleep," she says with a laugh.

35 to 40 small beets or 15 large beets
2 cups sugar
2 cups water
2 cups white vinegar
1 teaspoon ground cloves
1 teaspoon whole allspice
1 tablespoon ground cinnamon
1 teaspoon whole cloves

**In a kettle,** cook the beets until tender. Dip in cold water and peel off the skins. Slice ¼ inch thick or cut into quarters if using smaller beets. Pack tightly (snug but not bruising each other) into canning jars.

**In a large saucepan,** combine the sugar, water, vinegar, ground cloves, allspice, cinnamon, and whole cloves. Boil for 10 minutes and pour at once over the beets, leaving a ¾-inch headspace (the liquid should go no farther than the shoulder of the jar). Process in a boiling-water bath for 12 minutes. Remove immediately and cool on a rack.

Becky Quinn, Springfield, Missouri
*Ozark Empire Fair, Springfield, Missouri*

# Easy Dill Pickles

*1 quart*

Doris Laska has a 1½-acre garden and a roadside vegetable stand. Each year, she cans 100 quarts of vegetables and fruits, 50 jars of jams and jellies, and 50 jars of pickles.

**20 midget cucumbers (or larger cucumbers, sliced)**
**2 heads fresh dill**
**¾ cup apple cider vinegar**
**1½ tablespoons canning salt**

**Cut** the blossom ends off the cucumbers and leave a bit of the stem if it is there. (Do not peel.) Place 1 head of dill in a sterilized quart jar and pack with cucumbers. Add the vinegar, salt, and enough water to cover the cucumbers. Place another head of dill on top and seal. Process in a boiling-water bath for 10 to 15 minutes.

Doris Laska, Winona, Minnesota
*Minnesota State Fair, St. Paul, Minnesota*

---

## MINNESOTA STATE FAIR

### St. Paul, Minnesota

The Minnesota State Fair is one of the country's best-attended agricultural events, attracting more than 1.6 million people. This 12-day fair is held on a 310-acre fairground between St. Paul and Minneapolis. Competitions draw more than 35,000 entries vying for a share of more than $600,000 in prize money. Categories include livestock, fine arts, baked goods, fruits, vegetables, flowers, butter, cheese, bees, and honey products. The fair also has the Midwest's largest collection of food vendors—more than 300 concessions.

# Chili Sauce

*12 pints*

1 peck (8 quarts) tomatoes, cored, peeled, and chopped
1 pound celery, coarsely chopped
½ teaspoon ground cloves
3 tablespoons ground cinnamon
1 box (1 pound) brown sugar
1 quart apple cider vinegar
1 quart chopped onion
3 green bell peppers, chopped
8 hot peppers (preferably 'Hungarian Hot Wax'), coarsely chopped
3 cloves garlic, minced
1 tablespoon powdered mustard
¼ cup salt

**Combine** all the ingredients in a large pot. Cook over low heat until thick, about 2½ hours, stirring to prevent scorching. Pour into hot, sterilized jars. Seal the jars and process in a boiling-water bath for 15 minutes.

Mary Hartman, Canfield, Ohio
*Canfield Fair, Canfield, Ohio*

# CANFIELD FAIR

~

## Canfield, Ohio

The Canfield Fair is one of the oldest fairs in the country, and people in Mahoning County are proud of it. For the 125th anniversary in 1971, they published a detailed history of the fair, and for the 150th birthday in 1996, they published a cookbook packed with prizewinning recipes. In the history of the Canfield Fair, titled *The Time of Your Life* (Web-Graphics, Inc., 1971), author Howard C. Aley remembers his early days at the fair, "peering into tents, tramping the midway, cheering a favorite trotter, applauding a high-wire artist, or thumping a huge pumpkin." Now there are 16 paved midways filled with rides, games, and food concessions. Performers such as Willie Nelson and the Beach Boys entertain the crowd. You also can enjoy a real agricultural fair, with 4-H exhibits and competitions, talent shows, and harness races.

# Tammy's Tomato Ketchup

*3 pints*

When Tammy Reiss makes this recipe, she always uses homemade tomato purée. Here is how she makes her purée: Use ripe, juicy tomatoes. Wash and core. Chop into pieces and simmer until soft. Put through a food mill or strainer. Cook slowly until thick, stirring often to prevent sticking. While hot, pour into pint jars and process in a boiling-water bath.

> **2 quarts tomato purée**
> **1⅓ cups white vinegar**
> **½ cup sugar**
> **2 teaspoons whole allspice**
> **2 cinnamon sticks**
> **1 teaspoon whole cloves**
> **1½ teaspoons paprika**
> **1 teaspoon powdered mustard**
> **1 teaspoon salt**
> **1¼ teaspoons cayenne pepper**

**Combine** the tomato purée, vinegar, and sugar in a large saucepot. Tie the allspice, cinnamon sticks, and cloves in cheesecloth. Add to the tomato mixture. Add the paprika, mustard, salt, and cayenne and cook slowly until thickened, about 45 to 60 minutes. Stir frequently to prevent the ketchup from sticking. Remove the spice bag. Pour the ketchup into hot jars, leaving a ¼-inch headspace. Adjust the caps. Process in a boiling-water bath for 15 minutes.

Tammy Reiss, Moore, Oklahoma
*Oklahoma State Fair, Oklahoma City, Oklahoma*

For kitchen tips and more recipes, go to www.almanac.com/food.

# Tammy's Apple Jelly

*5½ pints*

Tammy Reiss says that cooking is one of the things she enjoys most. She has won blue ribbons three times with her apple jelly. "The one time I did not take first place with this recipe was when I decided to take a shortcut with skimming the foam. I added a dollop of butter, which is supposed to take care of the foam. But it made the jelly cloudy. This year I told myself no shortcuts and went back to skimming the foam, and I got another blue ribbon."

- **5 pounds apples**
- **5 cups water**
- **9 cups sugar**
- **1 package (1¾ ounces) powdered pectin**

**Remove** the stems and blossom ends from the apples. Cut into small pieces (do not peel or core). Place in a large pot with the water. Bring to a boil, reduce the heat, cover, and simmer for 10 minutes. Crush the cooked apples with a potato masher and simmer for 5 minutes more.

**Pour** the apple mixture into cheesecloth and let drain into a cooking pot until the dripping stops. Press very gently to get the last few drops of juice. Measure the juice and add water if necessary (no more than ½ cup) to make 7 cups.

**Measure** the sugar into a bowl. Stir the pectin into the apple juice and bring to a full rolling boil, stirring constantly. Add the sugar to the juice and return to a full boil. Cook for 2 minutes, stirring constantly. Remove from the heat and skim off the foam. Immediately ladle into ½-pint jars and seal. Invert the jars for 5 minutes, then turn upright.

Tammy Reiss, Moore, Oklahoma
*Oklahoma State Fair, Oklahoma City, Oklahoma*

# Pickled Watermelon

*2 pints*

9 cups water
½ cup salt
11 cups watermelon pieces (cut from rind, seeded, and
    cut into 1-inch cubes)
2½ cups white vinegar
5 cups sugar
1 cinnamon stick
¼ teaspoon ground ginger
2 tablespoons lemon juice

**In a large bowl,** stir the water and salt together. Add the watermelon and let stand overnight.

**Drain** the watermelon, rinse, and drain again. In a large saucepan, combine the vinegar, sugar, cinnamon stick, ginger, and lemon juice. Bring to a boil and add the watermelon. Return to a boil and simmer for 20 minutes. Remove the cinnamon stick. Loosely pack the watermelon into jars. Return the syrup to a boil and boil for 30 minutes. Pour over the fruit in the jars and seal. Process in a boiling-water bath for 15 minutes.

Shirley Barnes, Puyallup, Washington
*Western Washington Fair, Puyallup, Washington*

For kitchen tips and more recipes, go to www.almanac.com/food.

# Kiwi Freezer Jam

*6 cups*

Mary Schmaltz reminds cooks to keep these rules in mind when making jam: Don't double jam recipes and don't reduce the amount of sugar. Doing either of these things may result in having liquid jam. Also, if you are canning, consider your altitude and add 1 minute of cooking time for each 1,000 feet of altitude. (Note: Peel the kiwi fruit and remove the hard white core. Cut into cubes and mash with a potato masher. Do not purée.)

> 2¼ cups mashed kiwi fruit (about 9 kiwis; see note above)
> 4 cups sugar
> 1 pouch (3 ounces) liquid pectin
> ¼ cup lemon juice

**Prepare** the containers by rinsing with hot water. Use plastic containers or small canning jars with lids. Put the kiwi in a large bowl. Gradually stir in the sugar. Mix well and let stand for 10 minutes, stirring occasionally. Meanwhile, in a small bowl, combine the pectin and lemon juice. Add to the fruit mixture and gently stir (do not beat in air) for 3 minutes. Pour into the containers, leaving a ½-inch headspace. Put on the lids. Let stand at room temperature for 24 hours. The jam will keep in the refrigerator for up to three weeks or in the freezer for up to one year.

Mary Schmaltz, Pueblo, Colorado
*Colorado State Fair and Exposition, Pueblo, Colorado*

# Harvest Honey Fruit Spread

*2½ pints*

Annette Burmeister notes that any combination of fresh or frozen summer fruits totaling 4 cups (after being crushed or mashed) will work. She says, "I used half strawberries for the prizewinning batch and got a very pretty dark red color. I have made the spread with a greater proportion of cherries and blueberries and gotten a deep purple color—equally tasty." Annette started experimenting with honey recipes when she had a beehive that produced more than 10 gallons of honey each year. (Note: You may substitute frozen fruit. Just thaw and mash.)

> 2 cups crushed fresh strawberries
> 1 cup crushed fresh peaches
> ½ cup crushed fresh blueberries
> ½ cup crushed fresh sweet cherries
> 1 package (1¾ ounces) powdered pectin
> 2 cups honey
> 2 tablespoons fresh lemon juice

**Combine** the strawberries, peaches, blueberries, cherries, and pectin in a heavy saucepan. Bring to a full rolling boil over medium heat, stirring constantly. Cook for 1 minute. Add the honey and lemon juice. Return to a rolling boil and cook for 5 minutes, stirring constantly. Remove from the heat and skim off the foam. Ladle into sterilized jars, seal, and process in a boiling-water bath for 10 minutes.

Annette Burmeister, Lakeville, Minnesota
*Minnesota State Fair, St. Paul, Minnesota*

For kitchen tips and more recipes, go to www.almanac.com/food.

# Violet Infusion Jelly

*4½ pints*

Mary Ann Brahler has earned more than 30 ribbons for her canned goods. She is an organic gardener who lives in a solar-heated home on 36 acres in New Jersey. She says. "I want to remind people that New Jersey is an agricultural state, not just an extension of New York City." New Jersey's state flower is the violet, which Mary Ann frequently uses in cooking, making violet vinegar, violet syrup, and candied violets. She picks her violets in a field at an abandoned farm near her home and encourages cooks to find a pesticide-free source.

**3 cups violet flowers, stems removed**
**3⅓ cups distilled water**
**1 package (1¾ ounces) powdered pectin**
**4 cups sugar**

**Place** the flowers in a jar. Boil the water and pour over the flowers. Let steep for 24 hours.

**Strain** the infusion through a cheesecloth-lined strainer. Allow the liquid to drain fully without pressing the blossoms. (Pressing will make the jelly cloudy.) Discard the blossoms. In a large saucepan, bring the violet infusion and pectin to a full rolling boil. Add the sugar and stir well. Bring back to a rolling boil and cook for 1 minute. Remove from the heat and skim off the foam. Ladle into ½-pint jars, seal with lids, and process in a boiling-water bath for 10 minutes.

Mary Ann Brahler, Milford, New Jersey
*Flemington Agricultural Fair, Flemington, New Jersey*

# Tomato-Basil Jam

*2½ pints*

5 or 6 large ripe tomatoes, peeled, seeded,
   and finely chopped
¼ cup lemon juice
3 to 4 tablespoons coarsely chopped fresh basil
3 cups sugar, divided
1 package (1¾ ounces) powdered fruit pectin
   for lower-sugar recipes

**Place** the tomatoes in a kettle. Bring to a boil, reduce the heat, cover, and simmer for 10 minutes. Add the lemon juice and basil. In a small bowl, combine ¼ cup of the sugar and pectin and add to the tomatoes. Heat to a full rolling boil, stirring constantly. Add the remaining 2¾ cups sugar. Return to a rolling boil and cook for 1 minute, stirring constantly. Remove from the heat and skim off the foam. Ladle the jam into hot, sterilized ½-pint canning jars, leaving a ¼-inch headspace. Seal with lids and process in a boiling-water bath for 5 minutes.

Mary Ann Brahler, Milford, New Jersey
*Flemington Agricultural Fair, Flemington, New Jersey*

# Appendix

## List of Fairs, Festivals, and Cook-offs

*Note: Please verify all information before making plans to attend these festivals or ordering cookbooks.*

### ARIZONA

**Phoenix**
*Arizona State Fair*
1826 W. McDowell Road
Phoenix, AZ 85007
(602) 252-6771

### CALIFORNIA

**Gilroy**
*Gilroy Garlic Festival*
Gilroy Garlic Festival Association
P.O. Box 2311
7473 Monterey Street
Gilroy, CA 95020
(408) 842-1625

**Holtville**
*Holtville Carrot Festival*
Holtville Chamber of Commerce
101 West Fifth Street
Holtville, CA 92250
(760) 356-2923

**Indio**
*National Date Festival*
Fairgrounds Office
46350 Arabia Street
Indio, CA 92201
(760) 863-8247

**San Juan Capistrano**
*World's Championship Chili Cook-off*
International Chili Society
P.O. Box 1027
San Juan Capistrano, CA 92693
(877) 777-4427

**Stockton**
*Stockton Asparagus Festival*
311 E. Main Street, Suite 204
Stockton, CA 95202
(209) 644-3740

### COLORADO

**Pueblo**
*Colorado State Fair and Exposition*
State Fairgrounds
Pueblo, CO 81004
(719) 561-8484

### DELAWARE

**Georgetown**
*Delmarva Chicken Festival*
Delmarva Poultry Industry, Inc.
RD 6, Box 47
Georgetown, DE 19947
(302) 856-9037

*Delaware (continued)*

**Harrington**
*Delaware State Fair*
P.O. Box 28
Harrington, DE 19952
(302) 398-3269

## DISTRICT OF COLUMBIA

*National Chicken Cooking Contest*
P.O. Box 28158 Central Station
Washington, DC 20038
Fax: (202) 293-4005

## GEORGIA

**Perry**
*Georgia National Fair*
P.O. Box 1367
Perry, GA 31069
(418) 987-3247

**Vidalia**
*Vidalia Onion Festival*
100 Vidalia Sweet Onion Dr.
Vidalia, GA 30474
(912) 538-8687

**Vienna**
*Big Pig Jig*
Dooly County Chamber of Commerce
P.O. Box 308
Vienna, GA 31092
(229) 268-8275

## IDAHO

**Boise**
*Idaho Beef Cook-off*
Idaho Beef Council
242 S. Cole Road
Boise, ID 83709
(208) 376-6004

**Shelley**
*Dutch Oven Cook-off*
*Idaho Spud Day*
Shelley Chamber of Commerce
P.O. Box 301
Shelley, ID 83274
(208) 357-3390

## ILLINOIS

**Morton**
*Pumpkin Festival*
Morton Chamber of Commerce
415 W. Jefferson Street
Morton, IL 61550
(888) 765-6588

## INDIANA

**Indianapolis**
*Indiana State Fair*
1202 E. 38th Street
Indianapolis, IN 46205
(317) 927-7500

## IOWA

**Des Moines**
*Iowa State Fair*
P.O. Box 57130
Des Moines, IA 50317
(515) 262-3111

## KANSAS

**Lenexa**
*Spinach Festival*
Lenexa Historical Society
14907 W. 87th Street Parkway
Lenexa, KS 66215
(913) 492-0038

## LOUISIANA

**Bridge City**
*Gumbo Festival*
P.O. Box 9069
Bridge City, LA 70096
(504) 436-4712

**Colfax**
*Louisiana Pecan Festival*
P.O. Box 78
Colfax, LA 71417
(318) 627-5196

## MAINE

**Machias**
*Machias Wild Blueberry Festival*
P.O. Box 265
Machias, ME 04654
(207) 255-6665

**Pittsfield**
*Central Maine Egg Festival*
P.O. Box 82
Pittsfield, ME 04969
(207) 257-4209

**Rockland**
*Lobster Festival*

Rockland-Thomaston Area Chamber
of Commerce
P.O. Box 552
Rockland, ME 04841
(207) 596-0376

**Windsor**
*Common Ground Country Fair*
Maine Organic Farmers and Gardeners
Association
P.O. Box 170
Unity, ME 04988
(207) 568-4142

## MARYLAND

**Crisfield**
*National Hard Crab Derby*
Crisfield Area Chamber of Commerce
P.O. Box 292
Crisfield, MD 21817
(410) 968-2500

**Leonardtown**
*National Oyster Cook-off*
*St. Mary's Oyster Festival*
Department of Economic and
Community Development
P.O. Box 653
Leonardtown, MD 20650
(301) 475-4404

## MASSACHUSETTS

**Bolton**
*Bolton Fair*
P.O. Box 154
Bolton, MA 01740
(978) 779-6253

*Massachusetts (continued)*

**Plymouth**
*Cranberry Harvest Festival*
Cape Cod Cranberry Growers' Association
3202 B Cranberry Highway
E. Wareham, MA 02538
(800) 698-5636

## MICHIGAN

**Detroit**
*Michigan State Fair and Exposition*
1120 W. State Fair Avenue
Detroit, MI 48203
(313) 369-8250 x54

**Traverse City**
*National Cherry Festival*
109 Sixth Street
Traverse City, MI 49684
(231) 947-4230

## MINNESOTA

**Deer River**
*Deer River Community Wild Rice Festival*
Deer River, MN 55636
(218) 246-8195

**St. Paul**
*Minnesota State Fair*
1265 North Snelling Avenue
St. Paul, MN 55108
(651) 288-4400

## MISSOURI

**Kansas City**
*Kansas City Barbeque Society Contest*

11514 Hickman Mills Drive
Kansas City, MO 64121
(816) 765-5891

**Springfield**
*Ozark Empire Fair*
P.O. Box 630
Springfield, MO 65801
(417) 833-2660

## NEW JERSEY

**Ringoes**
*Hunterdon County 4-H and
    Agricultural Fair*
P.O. Box 2900
Flemington, NJ 08551
(908) 782-6809

## NEW YORK

**Rhinebeck**
*Dutchess County Agricultural Society
Dutchess County Fair*
P.O. Box 389
Rhinebeck, NY 12572
(845) 876-4001

## OHIO

**Canfield**
*Canfield Fair*
P.O. Box 250
Canfield, OH 44406
(330) 533-4107

**Columbus**
*Ohio State Fair*
717 E. 17th Avenue
Columbus, OH 43211
(614) 644-3247

For kitchen tips and more recipes, go to www.almanac.com/food.

## OKLAHOMA

**Oklahoma City**
*Oklahoma State Fair*
P.O. Box 74943
Oklahoma City, OK 73147
(405) 948-6700

## PENNSYLVANIA

**Kennett Square**
*Mushroom Festival*
P.O. Box 1000
Kennett Square, PA 19348
(610) 925-3373

## RHODE ISLAND

**Charlestown**
*Charlestown Seafood Festival*
Charlestown Chamber of Commerce
P.O. Box 633
Charlestown, RI 02813
(401) 364-4031

## SOUTH DAKOTA

**Sioux Falls**
*Sioux Empire Fair*
W. H. Lyons Fairgrounds
4000 W. 12th Street
Sioux Falls, SD 57107
(605) 367-7178

## TENNESSEE

**Lynchburg**
*Jack Daniel's Cook-off*
P.O. Box 199
Lynchburg, TN 37352
(931) 759-4221

## TEXAS

**Crystal City**
*Crystal City Spinach Festival*
P.O. Box 100
Crystal City, TX 78839
(830) 374-3161

**Dallas**
*State Fair of Texas*
P.O. Box 150009
Dallas, TX 75315
(214) 565-9931

## VERMONT

**Enosburg Falls**
*Vermont Dairy Festival*
P.O. Box 34
Sheldon, VT 05483
(802) 933-5921

## VIRGINIA

**Salem**
*Salem Fair*
P.O. Box 886
Salem, VA 24153
(540) 375-3004

## WASHINGTON

**Puyallup**
*Western Washington Fair*
P.O. Box 430
Puyallup, WA 98371
(253) 841-5045

# Index